"Radiant . . . [Schaefer never lapses into sentim pain makes *Grand* a fresh and engaging read. It is a wise, funny acknowledgment that we are not always in control—and that growth is most likely to happen when we let go."

—*BookPage*

"[Schaefer]'s certainly got a sensibility that—despite its obvious authenticity—might have been expressly tailored for the times."

—*The Guardian*

"In alternating chapters, and with plenty of heart, Schaefer traces the impact of a decades-old family scandal on her contemporary life in *Grand*."

—*Bustle*

"This is a funny, complicated book about a simple trip to the Grand Canyon that ends up unearthing some hilarious truths about its author, Sara Schaefer. I don't even think she was ready for the upheaval, and she captures all of the confusion, beauty, and ultimate growth in brilliant prose. Go deep with this one."

—Patton Oswalt, author of
Zombie Spaceship Wasteland

"I may be a tad biased, as I've been witness to Sara's career for well over a decade now, but this book is fantastic. Its conversational and honest style feels as though you're wrapped up in a big hug by a friend who makes it safe for you to reveal the most inner secrets of your life. I'm so proud of *Grand*, and it confirms what I knew years ago: Schaefer is a true talent, a strong writer, and has a delightful voice that we need to hear more of. This is just the beginning."

—Phoebe Robinson, author of
You Can't Touch My Hair

"I already knew from her comedy that Sara Schaefer is one of the funniest, smartest, bravest ones out there. But I didn't understand just how deep the funny/smart/brave went until I went with her on this wild river descent into the Grand Canyon and her own secret family history. This is a Class 1,000 rapids of a memoir and I urge you to take the ride."

—John Hodgman, author of
Vacationland

"I already knew Sara was a great comedy writer. In *Grand*, she reveals herself to be a great author as well. Through her trip down a crack in the earth's skin, Sara cracks open her own skin and lets her insides spill onto the page. *Grand* is funny, sweet, heartbreaking, vulnerable, and powerfully written. You'll tear through it at the speed of a Class X rapid."

—Moshe Kasher, author of
Kasher in the Rye

"Damn funny and damn poignant . . . Schaefer takes us on a wild, hilarious, and moving ride through the stirring, scenic Grand Canyon and the turbulent rapids of her own soul. It's one hell of a good trip!"

—Ed Helms

"Sometimes you have to go all the way to the bottom of the Grand Canyon to find your footing, and sometimes you just need the right book. In this vulnerable, hilarious, and nostalgic reflection, Sara plunges us into some of life's wildest, most painful, and most relatable circumstances, all while making sure our life vest is on tight."

—Abbi Jacobson, author of
I Might Regret This

sara schaefer

grand

a memoir

gallery books

new york   london   toronto   sydney   new delhi

G

Gallery Books
An Imprint of Simon & Schuster, Inc.
1230 Avenue of the Americas
New York, NY 10020

First Gallery Books trade paperback edition May 2021

For information about special discounts for bulk purchases, please contact Simon & Schuster Special Sales at 1-866-506-1949 or business@simonandschuster.com.

The Simon & Schuster Speakers Bureau can bring authors to your live event. For more information or to book an event, contact the Simon & Schuster Speakers Bureau at 1-866-248-3049 or visit our website at www.simonspeakers.com.

Interior design by Davina Mock-Maniscalco

Manufactured in the United States of America

10 9 8 7 6 5 4 3 2 1

Library of Congress Cataloging-in-Publication Data

Names: Schaefer, Sara Carole, 1978- author.
Title: Grand : a memoir / Sara Schaefer.
Description: New York : Gallery Books, 2020.
Identifiers: LCCN 2020010122 (print) | LCCN 2020010123 (ebook) | ISBN 9781982102210 (hardcover) | ISBN 9781982102234 (ebook)
Subjects: LCSH: Grand Canyon (Ariz.)—Description and travel—Anecdotes. | Schaefer, Sara Carole, 1978—Travel—Arizona—Grand Canyon. | Schaefer, Sara Carole, 1978—Family. | Schaefer family—Anecdotes. | Women comedians—New York (State)—New York—Biography—Anecdotes. | Comedians—New York (State)—New York—Biography—Anecdotes.
Classification: LCC F788 .S27 2020 (print) | LCC F788 (ebook) | DDC 917.91/320453092—dc23
LC record available at https://lccn.loc.gov/2020010122
LC ebook record available at https://lccn.loc.gov/2020010123

ISBN 978-1-9821-0221-0
ISBN 978-1-9821-0222-7 (pbk)
ISBN 978-1-9821-0223-4 (ebook)

For Lovie

chapter

one

"So, what are we talking? Maybe a couple of Class III rapids . . . but mostly flat river, right?" I inched my car forward along a brutal Los Angeles commute and waited for my younger sister, Ross, who was on speaker, to respond.

I thought of Wyoming. Over a decade earlier, I had experienced my first and only whitewater rafting trip—a thirty-minute dabble for tourists in the Yellowstone River. There's a photo of me from that day as we navigated a modest, Class II rapid. My face is overcome with terror, red and shrieking, as if I am about to die in a plane crash. It's a hilarious picture, not only because of the contrast of my reaction to everyone else's (they're all weeee! and woohoo!), but also because it looks like I'm terrified of a lazy river.

Ross's voice wavered slightly.

"Uh . . . I think there are going to be some pretty big rapids."

"But no Class V rapids, right?" I wasn't sure what constituted a Class V rapid, but I knew it was tough stuff. "They don't let regular people do those."

More silence.

"Sara, it's the Colorado River."

"Well, we'll be wearing helmets, so it will be fine."

"Helmets? Sara, no."

It was at this point that I realized I had no idea what I had gotten myself into.

———

From the moment we confirmed the trip, Ross had been focused on the packing list, which I had yet to even think about. Not because I wasn't excited or didn't care. For the past two years, I had been traveling somewhere for my comedy career every week, and once I booked the flight, rental car, and hotel, I wouldn't look at the details again until the day before departure.

But this was not an overnight trip to do a show at some

random college in suburban St. Louis. This was an eight-day whitewater rafting and camping trip through the Grand Canyon. The plan came together after I announced to my family that, during the year of my fortieth birthday, I wanted to take a one-on-one trip with each of them. My older sister, Cristy, and I would tour some California wineries; my older brother, Jay, and I would hit New Orleans; Dad and I would have a staycation at his new condo in Longboat Key, Florida. Ross and I decided to do something a bit more bucket-listy.

I am a birthday scrooge, and that's because I think my birthday is absolutely stupid. I don't understand why other adults don't think their birthday is stupid, either. When I see a novel-length post on social media about how "crazy" it is to be turning thirty-two, my eyes go dead. This birthday ennui isn't as a result of some sort of childhood trauma in which one of my family members was killed by a balloon animal. I am a birthday scrooge because I generally hate parties (far too noisy), and also because I was born in July. A July birthday means never getting a school celebration or your locker decorated, and, because most people are on vacation, very few of my already small circle of friends could attend my parties.

On top of this, Ross was born just eighteen months after me, and we were raised as a unit. Everyone called us "The

Girls." (Cristy, six years older than me, was apparently a full-grown woman already, and was not included.) Anything that affirmed me as an individual, separate from The Girls, was interpreted by Ross as a personal attack and she reacted badly.

In my family, there were just enough kids (four) and emotions (four million) to make it hard to stay in the direct eyeline of my parents (two) for very long. Attention was a fossil fuel: we all desperately needed it to survive, we worried it might one day suddenly run out, and we were willing to go to war over it.

My siblings each had a strong position on the battlefront: Cristy was the oldest and a cherished leader and assistant parent. Jay was the only boy and a clever minister of fun. I was the second-middle, which was a real dud, tactically speaking. Ross, the baby, was the cutest child any of us had ever seen, and she wielded that power to get away with all sorts of naughtiness.

There is a picture from my sixth birthday party, held at the local Putt-Putt. In it, I am wearing a gray apron dress over a white puffy shirt. I am proudly holding my favorite doll, Penny, and looming behind me is a large Putt-Putt sign. It had a white rectangle marquee, and in it, black letters read HAPPY BIRTHDAY, SARA! Seeing my name up there made me feel like the most important person in the world, and it was

4

the precise reason I had chosen to have my birthday party at Putt-Putt. I knew from past parties that part of the package was getting to see your name in lights. But even with a gigantic sign in the sky proclaiming it was *my* day, if you look at the picture closely you can see two legs directly behind mine, and the outline of a little blonde head peeking out from over my shoulder. It is Ross, my ever-present shadow, ever reminding me that it's her day, too.

Deep down, I actually liked sharing my birthday spot-light with Ross, as it made me feel like a benevolent queen. This was part of my strategy in the attention wars. As the second-middle, I had to employ the long game. My best shot would be through diplomacy and good behavior. It also helped that every time I received praise for being good, I simply felt better. Not better than others, just better than I normally did, which was caught in a tangle of worries over what I believed to be my responsibilities. These included everything from knowing how to correctly spell the word "chief," to managing the feelings of my stuffed animals (Penny was domineering and made the others jealous), to preventing the untimely death of myself and everyone around me.

Now, as I was staring down my fortieth birthday, I de-cided that this time I would allow myself to make a big deal out of my own birthday. I'd heard that when you turn forty, you "stop caring about what people think," and finally become a "warrior goddess hero boss queen."

Ross, too, was at a crossroads of sorts. After years of struggling with her health, she had finally found a treatment plan that was working. A trip like this would not have been possible for her a year before.

"The guides will cook gourmet meals for us," Ross said. She and Cristy had both settled not far from the Grand Canyon, in the mountain town of Flagstaff, Arizona. Ross knew someone at the rafting company and assured me this trip would be "luxury." "We'll have comfortable cots. Everything is included and taken care of." I took this to mean that it would be a relaxing vacation, not a rugged expedition. This is not to say I was completely oblivious—I knew that anything involving wilderness and water would be probably out of my comfort zone. And though Ross had worked at a 4-H camp in her twenties, she, too, would be experiencing something new. This was Big Nature, not the little nature we had known as kids.

In our upscale neighborhood in Midlothian, Virginia, a suburb of Richmond, we never encountered outdoors on the vast scale of the American West. I had no regular contact with a distant horizon, the way someone who grew up on a prairie or atop a mountain might. Our sunset splintered through trees, and I'd only heard of shooting stars. To us, nature was an empty field on Midlothian Turnpike, soon to be turned into a Walmart. Wildlife was a deer, soon to be turned into roadkill.

Danger was anything from the outside that had found its way into our house, like wasps. Their big butts would make a soft tapping sound against the wall, a sound that will make your skin fall off. Or, God forbid, the mouse. Mom feared mice and rats more than anything, but she summoned the courage to kill one that came into our house with a cast-iron skillet. She spoke of the incident in weighted tones, like an Oscar-winning actress describing how hard it was to pretend to be ugly.

It wasn't until decades later, when I visited Cristy in her new home in Arizona, that I saw Big Nature with my own eyes. There were pointy peaks, boundless pink desert, towering red rocks, and thousands of stars. We went to the south rim of the Grand Canyon on that trip, but I remember feeling disappointed. "It doesn't look real," I said. "It just looks like a photograph." The scale of it was beyond my comprehension, the north rim so far away it looked fuzzy. I wouldn't have been surprised if the entire landscape dropped to the floor to reveal that we were, in fact, on a movie set. Cristy had previously visited the bottom, on a camping trip to a Native American reservation in the canyon called Havasupai. She said, "The only way to truly understand the Grand Canyon is to go down into it."

Eighteen years later, I was going down into it. As the trip approached, Ross and I made a pact: I would protect her from her fears, and she'd protect me from mine.

The idea that we could shield each other from peril started when we were very young, lying in our bedroom at night. Because I was slightly older, it was my duty to protect us both. For years, right as I was beginning to drift off to sleep, Ross would call out, "Sara?"

"Yes, Ross." (I knew what was coming.)

"Will you protect me?" she'd beg.

(Sigh.)

She would continue, " . . . from the gremlins?"

(Long pause. An abyss of reluctance.) "Yes."

At this point, Ross would instantly fall asleep, and I'd be on my back, eyes wide, heart pounding, as I imagined a gremlin popping his head up at the end of my bed and licking my toes. As soon as her breathing hit that impossibly deep and frequent pace that only sleeping people can achieve, I would make myself light-headed mimicking it, in hopes that my body would soon follow and be done with my gremlin watch.

As we grew older, we learned to take turns protecting each other from whatever symbolic gremlin came our way. In the canyon, Ross's gremlins would be the creatures: spiders, scorpions, snakes, cougars, bats, bears. There are no bears at the bottom of the Grand Canyon, but what if one fell in and survived the fall? That bear is going to be pretty embarrassed and ready for some emotional eating.

I wasn't as concerned by the wildlife—my gremlin was the water. As a small child, I was so afraid of the ocean, I made my dad fill a baby pool with *fresh* water and drag it from the cottage we were renting all the way down to the beach. On the Colorado River, I would be perched atop a raft, my enemy below me. (My short trip on the Yellowstone had taught me that there are no seat belts on rafts. At the time, this shocked me.) I knew that there would be nothing keeping me out of those violent waters but my own feeble hands hanging on for dear life.

On an early August morning, I left Los Angeles to drive up to Flagstaff. Our trip launched in two days, so we would have some time to get organized together. Dad happened to be visiting that week, and he accompanied Ross and I on a last-minute supply run around town. As I was browsing camera accessories at the local camping outfitter, Ross appeared and put a twelve-inch hunting knife in my cart.

"We're going to need this," she said.

"For what?" I said, laughing.

"Bears. Cutting off my arm if it gets stuck in a rock. Or if we get into a *River Wild* type of situation." (*The River Wild* is the 1994 film in which Meryl Streep must save her family after a violent criminal, played by Kevin Bacon, takes them hostage on a raging river.)

"Are you ready to kill Kevin Bacon if it comes down to it?" I asked.

Ross's eyes became steely with resolve. "One hundred percent."

I figured this would be the moment she took the knife out of the cart, but she left it in, staring me down. I could tell she was partly serious, and that if I had said, *Yes, actually, I think we should bring this huge knife*, she would have purchased it without hesitation.

"Are we even allowed to bring knives?" I said. I looked at the packing list again, which, by this point, had become law in my head—deviating from it would surely spell trouble.

"I don't know and I don't care," Ross said, slightly bristled by my militance. "I'm bringing a knife." Thankfully, she ended up buying a smaller, more tastefully sized knife.

Our shopping complete, the three of us went for lunch.

Ross was fully amped. "Can you believe we are about to raft down two hundred and twenty-eight miles of the Colorado River?"

I gulped. *Two hundred and twenty-eight miles? What the hell?* I had somehow missed this figure in the literature. I pretended to be completely in the know.

"I know, it's crazy!" I said. Now that we were fewer than twenty-four hours out from launch, a real terror was forming in my gut.

As we waited for our food, I decided it would be best if I looked up videos of people rafting in the Grand Canyon on my phone.

Ross and Dad burst out laughing. "What? Sara, don't! This is only going to scare you more!"

"No," I said. "I need to know what to expect."

They were correct, of course—I should not have conducted a YouTube search for "Colorado River whitewater rafting" the day before I embarked on this journey. Because when you do a YouTube search for "Colorado River white-water rafting," the first videos that come up are the *notable* ones with the *most* views: the ones posted by adrenaline junkies with descriptors like "epic" and "total annihilation, bro!" and "near-death experience." I put the phone down.

"The boats are so big," Ross reminded me, "they are basically unflippable."

My brief search told me that she had no authority to make such a claim, not to mention a little film called *Titanic*, in which Leonardo DiCaprio tragically dies because of this exact line of thinking. But these facts were beside the point.

"I just don't want to look like a fool out there! Screaming like a child as we go over some dinky rapid!" I said.

They kept laughing, and this only made me panic more, because it reminded me that out in the wild with a group of strangers, I would not only be scared, but I might also be a total drag. I pictured the other people on the raft: a bunch of ripped outdoorsmen who collectively looked like they'd escaped a Mountain Dew commercial. I imagined them laughing at—or, even worse, annoyed by—my fear. I flashed back to every cool boy who'd ever mocked me for chickening out on the high dive or yelled at me for squeezing my eyes shut while trying to catch a fly ball. My nickname in middle school was Grandma, for God's sake. This was going to be a disaster.

"Look," my voice cracked, "If anyone makes fun of me for being afraid—I will—I cannot—!" My eyes started to well up.

Dad did his best to stifle his chuckles. "Aw, Bo," he cooed. (My family nickname is Bo, short for Bobara, which is short for Sara Sara Bobara Fonana Fanna Fofara Fee Fi Momara Sara. Obviously.) He smiled. "You girls are gonna have so much fun. Mom would be so proud of you."

Ugh, he's right. What is wrong with you?

The stakes were very low, but here I was acting like I was about to compete on *American Ninja Warrior*, untrained, in the nude.

Calm down.

12

But the truth was, I hadn't felt calm in a long time. On the surface, all seemed serene. My social media would tell you I was a working comedian with hobbies, love, a close family, and important opinions on trending topics. But inside, there was this impossibly tight knot, hissing at me, suffocating me, sucking the joy out of almost everything I did.

Stop it. Be happy. Be grateful. Be normal, stupid.

"Hey," Ross said. "If anyone messes with you down there? I'll destroy them. I have a knife."

chapter

two

I sat on my twin bed, the small green piece of paper in my hands starting to turn soft from the sweat of my eight-year-old palms. Printed on the paper was a drawing of a turtle. The turtle was staring at me with a sassy expression on its face, its tongue offensively hanging out. Next to the turtle were the words "Talky Turtle!" Underneath, there was a line for a parent's signature. It was blank. I wondered if dying might be easier than getting it signed.

It would soon be time for dinner. I imagined us all sitting at the round table, the woven cane seats of our chairs creaking as we settled, and then held hands to say the blessing, as we did every night. We took turns saying the prayer. If Jay said it, he would say it as fast as he possibly could: "Dear-GodThankYouForThisFoodBlessItToOurBodiesInJesus-NameWePrayAmen." If Dad said it, he'd take his sweet time, fancying up the language: "Please bless this food to the nourishment and sustenance of our bodies." This is when Jay, if you were unlucky enough to be sitting next to him, would start caressing the inside of your hand with his middle finger, as lightly as he possibly could. This was intended to make you laugh, and thus break the sacred silence of the blessing. It always worked.

"Zip it!" Dad would snap.

This is how dinner usually began, and often it would end with Jay getting sent to his room because he couldn't resist making Ross and I laugh. Manners were important in our house. We always had to say "Yes ma'am" and "No sir," and during mealtime, it was elbows off the table, eat over your plate, and do not reach for the biscuit bowl—instead, we were to ask, "Can someone please pass the biscuits?" And when you were finished with your meal, you were to ask, "May I please be excused?" At this point, Dad would survey your plate and decide if you had eaten enough of whatever dish he knew you hated. One New Year's Day, I sat at the dinner table alone for close to thirty minutes after everyone else had left, staring down two black-eyed peas. Black-eyed peas simply look wrong, and the sight of them made me gag. Mom demanded I eat them because if I didn't, it would bring an entire year of bad luck. For Dad it boiled down to a battle of man versus picky eater. I had initially refused to eat even one, so as punishment, he upped the ante to two, and I could not budge until they were both in my stomach. Eventually, I swallowed them whole like pills.

Tonight, I imagined, instead of Jay getting banished to his room for misbehaving, it would be me. That is, if I told them about Talky Turtle during dinner. What if I waited until after dinner? Or the next morning? Or the next life? I was scared of so many things growing up (the aforementioned water and gremlins, but also dogs, comets, the Easter Bunny, nuclear war, and jumping from heights greater than twelve inches—this is not an exhaustive list), but absolutely nothing terrified me more than Getting In Trouble.

In the first grade, I would hold in my pee for as long as possible in an attempt to minimize visits to the bathroom at school. This was because I had imagined a worst-case scenario in which I was literally caught with my pants down during a fire drill. In my mind, being in the bathroom would cause my fire drill partner, Aimee Jennings, to wander off looking for me and disappear forever. This of course would result in my immediate arrest and a hefty prison sentence.

Best to just hold it in. It should come as no surprise to you that, several weeks later, I shit my pants at school.

In the third grade, my teachers introduced a clever disciplinary system—if you got caught doing something bad, you got a little colored piece of paper with an animal printed on it. Runny Roo was a kangaroo that got caught running inside, Distracted Donkey was a donkey that wasn't displaying good listening skills. I liked it. The system was easy to follow, and I appreciated the creative touch.

One day, the unimaginable happened.

"Sara!" Mrs. Dressel shouted my name across the classroom. "Quiet!"

And with that, she walked to my desk and slapped down a Talky Turtle. I was instantly in total panic—not only because I was Getting In Trouble at school, but because you had to get your parents to *sign the demerits* and bring them back the next day. I was going to have to tell my mom and dad that I was a Talky Turtle.

I decided it would be best for everyone involved if I just signed it myself.

————

My early childhood was a heady time. We lived in an upscale subdivision called Salisbury, where the houses sat just far enough apart to suggest a certain level of wealth. Salisbury sits a few miles south of the James River, notably "below" the West End, where most of the old money of Richmond lived. Down here on the Southside, a younger upper class settled in the ambulating forest around the solidly preppy Salisbury Country Club.

The Schaefers were new to this lifestyle. Mom grew up poor with five siblings in Newport News. While her mother was in the maternity ward with her fifth child, my grandfather had a massive stroke and was brought in dead on arrival to the same hospital. Their lives were upended in that moment, and they lived in thirteen different places by the time Mom turned fifteen. One year, on Christmas Eve, they got evicted, and during the chaos, the movers knocked over their Charlie Brown–level Christmas tree and shattered all the ornaments.

Dad grew up in a blue-collar home in Richmond. His parents had a baby named Dickie who tragically died before turning one. Not long after, his mother adopted a baby from her nursing school friend who got pregnant out of wedlock. That baby was my dad, and they called him Billy. His parents drank too much, and they got mean when they did. He described Friday nights at the Schaefer house as "food fights, but not the *Animal House* fun kind." Dad grew up not knowing he was adopted, until, as a teen, his father told him in a stupor. The next morning, the old man took it back. He said, "I was drunk last night, I didn't mean what I said."

Mom and Dad met on a blind date when they were

nineteen. Dad didn't like the idea of a blind date but agreed to go because she had the same first name as him: Billie. Billy and Billie fell in love. The Vietnam War separated them for a while, but then they decided to get married in Las Vegas in July of 1969. Upon arrival, they discovered they did not have enough cash to cover the ceremony. Defeated, they began the drive back to Long Beach, where Dad was stationed with the Navy. But right before they slipped into the pitch-black desert, they saw a wedding chapel with a sign flickering: MASTERCARD ACCEPTED. The next day, they watched Neil Armstrong walk on the moon as newlyweds.

Dad started going by Bill, and they eventually moved back to Virginia, had four kids. He became a lawyer and built a successful business. She retired from nursing to raise us and make things look nice. In Salisbury, Mom developed a taste for the high life, and she liked to show it off. Her Porsche, complete with the license plate MOMS928, went with everything, but especially Dad's Porsche 911.

Mom loved shopping. She took the phrase "shop 'til you drop" literally. If you hadn't slipped a disc by the end of a day at the mall, you'd done it wrong. After, we would come home and do fashion shows for Dad, who loved seeing how happy we were to spend the money he earned. Mom's walk-in closet was a jungle of textures: beads, suede, fur, silk. It included both prim Laura Ashley dresses and chic 80s pieces like a metallic gold-plated object that we called the Wonder Woman belt. She would regularly call us in to get our opinion.

"Which shoe?" she'd ask, standing on one leg. We had to look at the shoe on her visible foot and size it up with the outfit on her body. And then she'd do a little hop and switch legs, revealing a second option on the other foot.

"I think the first one clashes," Mom would say.

Mom also loved entertaining, and always made sure our house looked and smelled great. She may have single-handedly moved potpourri markets with the amount she purchased. She loved decorating for every season. For Christmas, she went all out. She put electric candles in the windows and developed a system of hanging wreaths on the outside of each window with wide, luxurious velvet ribbon. The parties she threw for friends and Dad's clients were lavish. They hired a bartender and Mom dressed in head-to-toe sequins. Us kids had to stay upstairs, but I loved it, because the whole house was filled with a buzzy energy from the holiday cheer below. We would sneak down to get Cokes with cocktail cherries in them from the bartender. Back in our chambers, without adult supervision, we'd flop around on Jay's waterbed and listen to dirty stand-up comedy tapes of Eddie Murphy and Andrew Dice Clay.

The entire holiday season culminated on Christmas morning—when Mom and Dad gave the signal, we would scramble down the steps like horses released from a starting gate. Each child got their own corner of presents. Cristy, Ross, and I got mountains of toys and clothes, while Jay's stack was usually smaller. That's because he always got one really big present, like a pool table, or a Nintendo, or a pinball machine. It was bestowed upon him like a great responsibility, and he treated it as such—we came to know that a present for Jay was a present for us all. Once the tornado of wrapping paper and squealing died down, Mom gave a quick nod to the reason for the season by making us sing "Happy Birthday" to Jesus.

On the other side of each year was our summer vacation. Mom made sure they were decadent, too, with southerly destinations like the Grand Floridian at Disney World, or an oceanfront cottage on the Outer Banks of North Carolina. Dad loved surprising us at the end of vacation, stopping "to go to the bathroom" at a hotel in Colonial Williamsburg only to reveal we were staying for a few extra days.

We'd hit the road in our wood-paneled Dodge minivan, with a license plate that read FOR MOM. She packed the back like a Tetris game and hollowed out the inside by removing the middle seat, so that us kids could have room to play, nap, and immediately die if we were to get into a crash.

Once, while barreling down Interstate 95, we were going so crazy in the back of the minivan that Mom wrote something on a piece of paper and stuck it to the window with a piece of Juicy Fruit gum straight from her mouth. Cars honked and gave her the thumbs-up while she and Dad howled with laughter. At first, I couldn't see what the sign said, because I was so distracted by the gum. I was horrified that Mom would so flagrantly break the rules and put wet Juicy Fruit on a car window. If any of us had done that, we'd be in deep trouble. As I sat there in panic and disgust, I finally made out the words on the sign, visible through the thin, sunlit paper: PLEASE, TAKE OUR KIDS! Even though I was pretty sure Mom was joking and she didn't actually want to abandon us, I have held a searing hatred for chewing gum ever since.

Dad also loved dark humor. He would ceaselessly tease Ross and me about the family dog, Molly, referring to her as a "mangy mutt," which she was, but also as "a piece a dog meat," which scared us because it sounded like he was ready to throw her on the grill.

But there was also an austere side to him. Dad was constantly stressed about work. He'd sit on the plaid love seat in our corner den and throw his right foot up on the opposite knee, forming a triangle with his leg. The casualness of that pose contradicted the tightness of his face. His hand, in the shape of a gun, would hold up his clenched jaw while his glacial eyes fixed on some faraway apparition. I thought his whole head might shatter if I touched it.

Whatever was stressing him out was starting to choke

him, literally. His esophagus was spasming and making it difficult to swallow food. Our already tense dinners would be interrupted by the sounds of him coughing and gagging in the bathroom, and the problem eventually resulted in a terrifying trip to the emergency room. Thankfully, a quick procedure fixed the issue, but instead of alleviating the strain of our mealtimes, it only made him more militant.

"Chew it UP! You're going to choke!" he'd growl whenever we took too big a bite.

At his worst, we called him Bad Bill. Bad Bill sat steely-eyed while us kids frolicked around him. Huge fights would break out over seemingly small messes or simple misunderstandings. Mom could wield his temper over us, saying things like "Oh just you wait 'til Daddy gets home!" and then the sound of his Porsche vrooming into the driveway would send us scurrying. One time he was so mad at Ross and me, he came into our room at bedtime, lifted up the bottom half of my bed a few inches in the air, and slammed it down. Then he walked over to Ross and hit her on the head with a spoon. He was strict with Cristy, and his fights with Jay, now as tall as him, could get scary, but not as scary as his battles with Mom, because sometimes those would make him pack a bag and drive away. The sound of that vroom going in the other direction felt worse.

Bad Bill didn't sleep. I knew he wasn't sleeping, because my bedroom was above our corner den, and while on gremlin duty, I could hear him watching TV late into the night. One time I trotted downstairs to see what he was doing.

"Daddy, why are you still awake?" I asked.

"Because I can't sleep," he said grimly. "Go back to bed."

I knew something was wrong, but I did not know what. I could feel the stakes mounting, the faint smell of not-rightness curling in the air around us. This boat we were all in felt overloaded, and I was terrified of rocking it.

———————

It was time for me to sign the Talky Turtle. This was for the best—my parents had enough to worry about without dealing with my little slip. And besides, I would never make a mistake again, so what was one act of forgery just to smooth things out? Normally, Mom signed permission slips, so what if I signed my *dad's* name? They had no idea what his handwriting looked like! This was a genius idea. I found a pen and committed my first and only act of forgery.

Later that night, as I lay in bed, I became filled with worry about my clandestine operation. I replayed the entire sordid episode in my head again and again. Exhausted, I turned to Thumb.

Thumb was literally my thumb, and I sucked it. You shouldn't remember sucking your thumb. If you do, that means you did it for too long. I remember sucking mine, because I just finished off a quick session a few minutes ago. Thumb had the power to calm me when nothing else could. I loved Thumb. Thumb helped me fall asleep on many a night of anxious worrying and fear.

The next morning, I took my Talky Turtle forgery to school. Before handing it to my teacher, I examined my handiwork one more time. And wow, it was *really* good. *Just like Bill Schaefer's signature!*

Mrs. Dressel took one look at it and said, "Did you sign this yourself, Sara?"

That night, Dad sat me down. I braced for fury, but instead, what came was anguish. It was as if I had stabbed him in the heart.

"Bo, why did you do this?"

I could not conjure up whatever cute mojo Ross employed in times like this. Instead, I immediately started crying and said, "I didn't want to make anyone mad!"

He thought for a moment, and then said, "It would have been so much better if you had just owned up to it in the first place."

I'll never forget what he said next.

"All it takes is one little white lie. Then that lie turns into another lie. And then another lie. And then the lie is so big that you can't escape it."

chapter

three

It was 5:00 a.m. and dark when we took our seats on the charter bus outside a Marriott in Flagstaff. All morning I'd been riding waves of nausea.

There was no escaping the rafting trip now, and even though I knew I should be excited, I felt nothing but an all-over bad vibe I call The Doom. I've experienced bouts of The Doom my whole life, and it comes on so suddenly and with such force that it feels like a warning. But nothing bad ever happens after The Doom, and following each episode, I must accept once again that I do not have psychic abilities. The Doom is random.

On big days like this, though, it lingers. As I sat down on the bus, I couldn't help but examine it for meaning.

Is this a sign? Am I actually going through with this? I'm not cut out for this shit!

I looked around. The other people, to my relief, looked nothing like a Mountain Dew commercial. They appeared to be mostly couples, mostly older than us, and certainly not the intimidating adrenaline junkie types I had feared they would be. Ross and I introduced ourselves to the people sitting near us. Still, I felt queasy.

I needed to lighten the mood. I leaned over to Ross and said, "We have to establish ourselves. What if we stood up right now and took charge of the bus?"

She got it immediately.

"Listen up, assholes!" she said, as if patrolling the aisles, but quietly enough that only we could hear. "This is how it's gonna be!"

"You answer to *us!*"

"*We're* the cool ones!"

We giggled at the thought of us beginning our Grand Canyon trip with the attitude of pledge masters.

Soon, we were on our way. As we pulled out and onto the

highway, the bus was dead quiet. The sun bulged over the flat horizon.

The driver, a jolly older man, announced that he would play us a video about the Grand Canyon.

"This is my first time playing it for a group. Let me know what you think of it!"

The video showed wild footage of boats flying through the air and flipping in the massive rapids, set to a folksy fiddle, and there was a narrator with the voice of a campfire.

"Messin' about in boats. You could say that's what this whole thing is about. Boats. And rivers. And stories. There's a couple things you need to know about river stories. First off, they ain't short. Second, they're a little like rivers themselves. They tend to change some, as the years go by. And lastly, river stories are usually about ancestors. Now, on the river, an ancestor is anybody who ran the river before you did. So, meet the ancestors."

The first ancestor, according to the Hopi tribe, was a boy named Tiyo, who ran the river in a hollowed-out cottonwood log. The first non-Native people to explore the canyon were led by the one-armed Major John Wesley Powell in 1869. We learned about the Kolb brothers, Emery and Ellsworth, who were the first to make a film of the river. Buzz Holstrom made the first trip alone, in a wooden boat he built himself. Glen and Bessie Hyde mysteriously vanished, their boat found filled with their supplies and undamaged, creepily floating downriver as if their ghosts were still riding in it. Dr. Elzada Clover and Lois Jotter were the first women to run the river. By 1949, there was record of only about one hundred people running the Colorado River through the Grand Canyon.

A woman spoke on camera about her love for the canyon. She said, "I want to die down there."

"I . . . do not want that," Ross said.

Another woman said, "The canyon will take you apart and put you back together again." Now that was more like it. Going down into the canyon and being reborn in some way? The Doom suddenly lifted. Maybe down there I could find answers. I wasn't even sure of the questions, but in that moment I wanted to believe.

Outside the bus windows, the landscape gradually became more jagged. Red buttes jutted upward as the road began to twist downward. We made a final stop at an outpost in Marble Canyon, where a family of four joined us. I was both surprised and comforted to see they had two children with them, a pair of girls aged nine and eleven. *It can't be that dangerous if they let little kids do this!*

As we lingered around the bus, I checked my email and social media one more time. At dinner the night before, we had discussed the prospect of going eight days without a cellphone signal.

"If something were to happen to my kids, say," Ross said. "Y'all would find a way to let me know . . . right?"

Ross's friend, who had done the trip before, shook her head and said, "No. The only communication to the outside world is if it's a life-or-death situation."

"So, right," Ross continued, unfazed, "life or death, if something were to happen—"

"Life or death *in the canyon*," her friend corrected her. Ross's eyes widened.

Cristy jumped in, "Don't worry, Ross, I know people. We will find a way to get to you if we need to." I imagined Cristy convincing a park ranger to fly a helicopter down into the Grand Canyon to let us know that Ross's son was running a fever. She would speak in a highly persuasive dialect I call American Swunty (a language that is equal parts sticky sweet and downright cunty, popularized by white women across the South, handed down to us by our mother, and her mother before that), and get it done.

"Besides," I added, "*nothing* is going to happen! Stop imagining that!"

We finally made it to the river, and everyone got off the bus. Backpacks and duffles haphazardly strewn along the beach, we were each given dry bags, made of thick yellow rubber, to hold our stuff and keep it dry. The sleepy mood of the bus ride had shifted. Now, the anticipation was palpable. People snapped selfies, slathered on suntan lotion, chattered. The sky was stark blue against the contrast of the red cliffs surrounding us.

The four river guides were already there. They appeared to be young, strong, and already a little dirty. I guessed that if they had appeared too clean, I would be worried.

The lead guide, Ted, looked like he was born on a surfboard. He asked us to gather around.

"All right everybody! Welcome!" his voice was exactly as Keanu Reevesy as I imagined it would be.

Ted walked us through a few basics, including how to properly close our dry bags and affix our life jackets to our bodies.

As I buckled my vest, I worried it wasn't tight enough. Another river guide, Tyler, came over to help. Tyler's dark beard was a nice mountainy contrast to Ted's beachy look. He pulled at my life jacket like he was tightening a corset, and yes, it was kinda hot, but only because safety makes me horny.

"We know that some of you have diet restrictions," Ted continued, "but you might need to remind us of your needs as we're preparing meals. Don't be shy!"

Ross was one of those people. She had been very private

about her health stuff, so I was glad the guides were encouraging her to talk openly with them.

Other than that, Ted gave us surprisingly little information at this juncture, and only minimal notes about safety. We did not practice saving someone from drowning. We did not do a dry run of unflipping a boat. We did not learn CPR or how to amputate a leg in a pinch. All the guides seemed so casual about the entire thing; it both frightened and reassured me. They reminded me of how flight attendants behave during horrific turbulence. I always look at their faces. If they look calm while the plane feels like it's being ripped apart, then I guess there is nothing to worry about. *Or, maybe flight attendants, and these river guides, are top-tier lunatics?*

"Okay, it's time to get on the boats!" Ted yelled. *Already?*

Ted quickly explained where we could walk on the boats, how to balance ourselves on the slippery blue rubber, and which seats meant for a wetter ride. The front was the wettest and wildest, and all the way in the back there was a box you could perch upon, called "the princess seat," for those hoping for something drier.

I won't lie—I really wanted that princess seat, but I also didn't want to announce to the group that I was a giant coward so early. So I tugged at Ross's life jacket and whispered with the full urgency of my life depending on it,

"Let's sit in the middle-back. We *have* to get those seats!" I said "we," but I knew Ross would be the one staking our claim. She is always more comfortable pushing her way through a crowd of people to get what she wants.

Sure enough, Ross succeeded, sitting fourth back from the front and I behind her. Our lead boatman was Tyler. The second boatman was Matt, who had silky, long blond hair and the look of a Viking poet. The boat itself was made of thick, powder-blue rubber, about thirty-five feet long, capable of holding up to fourteen passengers. The center had a rectangular frame, the inner portion of which would hold our supplies and baggage under tarps. On either side, we would sit on padded storage lockers, and rest our feet on long inflated tubes that ran the length of the boat. The whole rig was hinged in the front and the back, so that the boat could actually bend and fold in the huge rapids ahead.

The other passengers on our boat included mostly young couples, a few solo travelers, and one older pair. The other boat was helmed by Ted and the fourth boatman, Jesse, a scrappy-looking fellow with a strawberry-blond buzz cut. Their passengers included the family of four, along with some other couples and solo riders.

As our rafts gently bumped against each other at the shore, Ted yelled out a safety tip: "You won't fall off if you're holding on!" explaining that you want to have a "two-hand hold" with each of your hands holding on to a rope or strap on opposing sides of your body. Thankfully, someone responded to this by asking my heart's deepest question.

"What if we fall off?"

Ted said, "You'll go for a little swim, but we'll get you out. But do not swim to the back of the boat. That's where the motor is."

Right, because that is how my body would be torn to shreds. Noted.

With that, the motors buzzed into gear and we launched off the shore. Ross and I squealed. *Here we go!* I still had a cellphone signal, so I took a selfie of Ross and me and sent it to our family. I made sure we looked cute, because I knew this would be the photo shown on the news if we died.

The water was flat, clear, and a deep blue-green. Tyler explained that the water was clear here because we were just on the other side of Glen Canyon Dam. It comes out clear because it's been sitting in a giant reservoir, allowing the sediment to settle to the bottom. This clarity would be short-lived, he said—soon, the sediment of side canyons and flash floods would muddy things up.

Minutes later, the water did indeed turn a chocolatey, reddish brown. As if on cue, my cellphone signal disappeared, too, and the river got a little choppier. There was no turning back now.

Someone joked, "The water looks like the Willy Wonka chocolate river!" Everyone laughed.

I leaned over to Ross and said, "I think it looks more like Yoo-hoo."

Matt and Tyler explained that the Colorado was named for its color: *Color* plus *rado*. To an untrained eye, the river might appear polluted. But here, this color is natural. The water is mixed with clay and worn rock and sand and hillside and tree dust from as far away as the tops of mountains, churning ever downward through this epic channel. It smelled like nothing I'd ever smelled before—a mix of fall leaves, wet metal, and expensive mud mask. Janet, a nurse, expressed concern over how we'd ever stay clean in this environment. I figured that all these minerals would be good for our skin and tried not to think about the possibility of tapeworms.

Matt was our geology expert. He explained that here we were, in terms of elevation, near the top of the canyon. As we traveled downriver, it would get deeper and deeper.

"Here's how you can remember the layers of the Paleozoic rock: Know The Canyon's History, Study Rocks Made By Time.

K, know, is for Kaibab Formation.

T, the, is for Toroweap Formation.

C, canyon's, Coconino Sandstone.

H, history, Hermit Shale.

S, study, Supai Group.

R, rocks, Redwall Limestone.

M, made, Muav Limestone.

B, by, Bright Angel Shale, and

T, time, is for Tapeats Sandstone."

"Will there be a quiz?" someone asked, and the raft erupted with laughter at the obvious joke.

I realized in that moment that there was something else about this trip that I hadn't yet considered. *I am going to be down here for eight days with a bunch of normies.* Comedians refer to anyone who is not directly involved in the comedy business as "normies," or "regular people." If this sounds condescending, it totally is, and I apologize. We comedians spend most of our time with other comedians or people who understand our weird, but not necessarily better, lives. We have a shorthand, a unique set of social rules and a group dynamic, and it can make us come across like complete assholes when we are in the company of the general population. I considered this, and worried that I was not going to be a team player. *Open yourself up to the experience, Schaefer,* I thought. *Remember what the lady in the video said: Let the canyon take you apart. Let your entire being become dismantled. Right now! Come apart! Do it!*

I shook my head like an Etch a Sketch, a technique I'd

developed over the years, to try to stop and clear the spiraling negative thoughts. *Stop. Look at the Grand Canyon. Look at those fucking rocks.*

The youngest, highest layer of those fucking rocks, Kaibab, is a pale orange. The word Kaibab means "mountain lying down," and it covers everything beneath it like a blanket. It is the youngest layer, a spry 250 million years old, just sitting on top like a spoiled teen, completely unaware of the vast and ancient foundation that came before it, thrusting it into the sunshine.

"Many people think that the Grand Canyon was simply carved by the waters of the river, but it is much more complex than that," Matt said. "Tectonic plates pushed the earth up and up, creating the plateau that the Colorado would cut through, revealing all these layers we see."

After the geology lesson, it was time for our first rapid, or as Tyler called it, "A little bump."

I clenched the ropes with all of my might as we headed over the tiny undulating hills. A few small splashes hit the people in the front, and everyone yelled "woohoo!" My scream was a little less exuberant, but thankfully I did not shriek as I had on the Yellowstone.

"How big of a rapid would you say that was?" I asked, needing a reference point.

"That was a two or a three . . . out of ten," said Tyler.

Down in the canyon, the scale for rapids is different than most rivers (most others use a scale of one to five). Each day, rapids fluctuate slightly in size, depending on the amount of water flow from the dam. Whole new rapids can be formed in an instant by landslides, flash floods, and rock fall. And the way you hit the rapid affects the experience, too.

During lunch, Ted explained that we would be practicing something called "Leave No Trace" camping. We were to leave nothing behind, not even crumbs of food. It doesn't matter if it's biodegradable—any small invasion of foreign materials could irrevocably damage the cryptobiotic systems in the soil.

This extended to our bodily functions, too. We were to pee in the river, and poop into a can. Before I could wonder if I had the leg strength, not to mention the aim, to deposit my leavings into a tiny can, Ted explained that they had devised a convenient and comparatively luxurious system called The Groover and not to worry, they'd teach us all about it at camp tonight. I started to guess that part of the river guides' strategy was to only give us information as we needed it. This was both smart and unsettling.

After lunch I had to pee, and I had yet to see any other women attempt it, so I wasn't sure how one goes about peeing in a river. Would I drop trou right there on the beach, remove my shoes and underwear, wade ankle deep, spread my legs, and just go for it? That seemed humiliating. Or would I need to swim downriver a mile to get some privacy, and then swim back? I decided to ask Tyler, thereby ending any fantasy that I could appear exotic and beautiful to my handsome guide.

"So, hey . . ." I said. "How *exactly* do you recommend I, a lady, pee in the river?"

"Wade out waist-deep and do it," he said. "Or, to feel a little more secure in the current, you can walk out beside the boat and hang on to it while you go. Like this."

I watched him wade out alongside the boat, and he started pulling on the ropes, acting like he was doing work.

"You can pretend to be checking the ropes!" He patted the side of the raft, satisfied with his fake work. "Yep! All good, nice and tight."

I laughed. Once he came back ashore, I took his place next to the boat. It was mentioned earlier that the water was 55 degrees, but it wasn't until now that I realized how shockingly cold that was, especially against the nearly 100-degree August desert heat. My pee warmed me. I appreciated the muddy hue of the water giving me a little more privacy as I urinated in front of twenty strangers nearby, but still, I did think about triumphantly yelling, "I'M PEEING!"

When I emerged, I told the other women in the group

that peeing was easy, and now that I was out in the dry sun, my wet clothes actually felt refreshing. One fear, though small, had been conquered.

Now, it was time to tackle a big one. There was no choice; that's where the river was taking us.

chapter

four

"It's all about choices," Dad often said, and every time, I wanted
to scream. It was his standard response to any moral or prac-
tical dilemma in our lives. Stressed about school? Maybe you
shouldn't have played video games for so long the night before.
It's all about choices. Wishing you could have ice cream? Should
have eaten the broccoli on your plate. *It's all about choices.*
Sprained ankle? Watch where you're going. *It's all about choices.*

But while the motto irritated me, I also latched on to it.
"It's all about choices" turned out to be quite the handy aid in
my obsessive need to be good.

One time, while riding in the minivan home from the dentist's office, I looked down and saw something horrific: a *Highlights* magazine from the waiting room. It was *in my hands.* And *it did not belong to me.* I had accidentally taken it with me, i.e. stolen it, i.e. committed grand larceny, i.e. thrown my entire life away. And for what? The chance to find the banana hidden in the colorful illustrated kitchen? I could not believe I had been so reckless.

You dummy. You chose to not pay attention. Now everything is ruined.

I demanded Mom turn around and take me back so I could return it. I remember my heart pounding as I walked up the steps to the office door. I had my speech prepared: *Yes, I stole the magazine, but I promise, it was not on purpose!*

The receptionist barely blinked when I put it back. But I felt my balance restored. One good choice had the power to erase a bad one.

Even though I still made mistakes, at least I could easily find the reason, run my fingers over it again and again to learn the lesson, and never make that bad choice again. I was weaving a tapestry of ethical codes and if I left even one thread loose, I might fall into an abyss of bad.

When I was about twelve years old, I made the mother of all good choices: I decided to enter into a personal relationship with Jesus.

My sister Cristy had introduced me to the idea. I idolized Cristy. She had dusty blonde hair and tan skin and tons of friends and talked to boys on the phone, all while making the honor roll. She showed me that being good while also being cool was possible.

Once, while Ross and I played badminton in the yard, Cristy and her friends suddenly came careening around to the back of the house and screeched the car they were driving to a halt. Jumping out, Cristy screamed at us, "GET INSIDE! HURRY!" as if some kind of apocalyptic acid tornado were about to hit. We rushed into the house and heard the sound of engines revving. Peeking out the front windows, we saw an entire motorcycle gang swarming in our semicircle driveway, popping wheelies, engines barking in a clear sign of aggression. Cristy explained to us that someone in the car had "waved at" the motorcycle gang and they started chasing them. (Cristy would later admit that her friend had cut them off.) After about a minute, the gang rode off, and Cristy and her friends collapsed into a pile of laughter. Dad, of course, was furious and went out looking for the gang (To do what? Physically fight a group of men on hogs?) and offered the girls some choice words about the choices that had led to this dustup.

I was both shaken and mesmerized by the energy of the incident. These girls had flirted with danger and it had actually been *fun* for them. I yearned for that freedom, and the bond it seemed to give them. I wanted her confidence and her older-ness. I wanted to be like Cristy.

And because Cristy went to church every Sunday, I followed.

All four of us kids were regulars at Winfree Memorial Baptist Church; my parents less so. Normally it's the parents who drag their kids to church, but Mom dropped us off. She and Dad were what us serious Christians called "CEOs— Christmas and Easter Ones," the type who only showed up on the big holidays, and the type who were definitely going to hell.

Cristy had left for college the previous summer, so someone had to take up the torch as the top Christian in the family. In order to do that, I had to level up.

Leveling up at a Baptist church is, well, baptism (it's in the name). Baptists, in theory, generally believe that faith is a matter between you and the Lord. That means that you decide if you want to "get dunked," as we called it. Baptists don't fool around with that sprinkle shit—how on earth are you going to wash the sin off with just a few drops of water? If you want to get clean, you have to take a whole bath.

The way it worked at Winfree is that when you were ready to commit your life to Christ you "went up to the front," meaning, you waited until the end of Sunday worship, when everyone was standing and singing the final hymn, and you approached the pulpit to announce your intentions. This was often a planned thing, coordinated by your parents and your Sunday school teacher when the time was right. But for me, it was totally impulsive. No one ever went up to the front on Christmas Eve, but I was really feeling the reason for the season that night.

Like Mom, I, too, loved Christmas. Christmas Eve service at Winfree was always enchanting—the sanctuary sparkled, we held candles, it was church *at night*. That year, I was hanging with my youth group pals in the balcony, whispering about what Christmas morning might bring us. I felt pretty in my purple dress. The world was filled with possibilities. The Holy Spirit grabbed me and whispered, "Now is the time. When no one is expecting it. You look fabulous in this soft lighting. Create a moment that they'll never forget. *Go up to the front, my child.*" And up to the front I went.

I chose Jesus that night, not out of some fear of going to hell. Even as a child, I was never interested in the "bus ticket to heaven" aspects of Christianity. (The idea that children born in a remote jungle of the Amazon would go to *eternal* hell, simply because they didn't know about Jesus, never sat right with me.) I was less concerned with what happens after you die, and more curious about freedom from the hell here on earth. I was looking for solutions to my tween problems, like: How do I feel accepted in the cruel halls of middle school? How do I be the *best* at being good? How do I get Eric Wilborn to like me? How do I become the center of one person's attention wholly and completely? Who will be all mine to love me for me in all my totality?

And also, how can I stop people from calling me Grandma, a nickname I earned by having the hobbies, muscle mass, and overall demeanor of an elderly woman?

At church, I was being offered a solution: Jesus. I ached for the love they said He delivered. While I was holding myself in cruel judgment for every choice I'd ever made, Jesus offered an alternative: grace. He loved and accepted me, Talky Turtles and all. His love was boundless, and incomprehensible, in that it could be infinitely focused directly at me, yet also shared with every other living thing. I could binge on his love without feeling selfish for stealing it away from someone else.

The next morning, I opened a small box atop my mountain of presents. As if my parents could sense my burgeoning infatuation with Christ, they had purchased me a gold necklace with a cross on it. It gleamed in the glow of the tree and all felt good.

I was good. My family was good.

Life was good.

Six weeks later, my parents called a family meeting on a dark night in Salisbury.

We'd never had a family meeting before.

As we sat arranged on the plaid furniture in the wood-paneled room, my dad faced us, built-in bookshelves dotted with country knickknacks looming behind him. Ross sat wide-eyed on Mom's lap. She wasn't quite old enough to look worried. Being twelve years old, I had an inkling this wasn't gonna be good. Jay definitely knew. Cristy held a tissue. (She *already* knew—hours earlier, my parents had picked her up from the University of Virginia, where she was a freshman. This had to be major if they went all the way out there to get her.)

When Dad finally spoke, his voice was like wispy cotton.

"I've done something wrong," he said.

I glanced at Mom. She was as dead-eyed as a mannequin.

Dad continued. The "something wrong" was inappropriate use of his clients' funds. I wasn't entirely sure what that meant, but it sounded serious. He explained that his business had been booming, and he had assumed, arrogantly, that it would continue to boom. It did not. When faced with an unexpected downturn, he looked around at the fancy life he'd built and was blinded by the fear of losing it. So he shifted money around, thinking he could put it back before anyone missed it. It spun out of control, and now, he couldn't live with the secret anymore. My father finished up by saying, "Tomorrow, I'm going to tell everyone the truth. I don't know what's going to happen. But I can promise you, we're going to start over, and we're going to rebuild."

My mind scanned. I knew the world was about to change, but I couldn't figure out how. I did not, and would not, for decades, fully understand what he had said.

(I did not know, until nearly thirty years later, that he was, in the months leading up to this moment, contemplating suicide. I did not know that earlier that day before the announcement, he had come home from work and checked the mail. I did not know that, while still in the car, he had opened up a birthday card from Cristy. It was nothing particularly dramatic, just a card from his oldest child away at school, wishing him a happy birthday, and saying how proud she was to be his daughter. I did not know that those words would cut him in two, and out from the fissure would come heaving sobs, as he sat in the driveway in his Porsche. I did not know that in that broken, bottomed-out place, he would say to himself, *I cannot live like this anymore. I would rather go to jail than live one more day with this secret. Whatever happens, it has to be better than this.* He went inside, confessed to Mom, and chose a new path.)

chapter

five

"Now," Ted said, as we reassumed our positions on the boats after lunch, "just downriver, we're going to hit our first big water. Have fun out there!"

"How big are we talking?" I asked Tyler, as we headed downstream, trying to sound only mildly curious, not quaking with terror.

"I'd say about an eight," Tyler said.

I grabbed Ross's leg.

"Oh god oh god oh god oh god," I said. *An eight already? Fuck!*

Ross squeezed my hand. I could tell by her grip that she was nervous, too.

Soon, we could hear the sound of rushing water. We came around a bend to see Ted's boat idling on the river ahead. I could see white water, but it still looked kind of flat from this distance. Tyler explained that we would watch the other boat go through first.

"This is House Rock Rapid," he said, "created by a debris flow out of Rider Canyon. You're going to want to hold on tight, the two-hand hold. Opposing sides."

"Scared!" I said to Ross in a little kid voice. It was a Schaefer family inside joke, the single word Cristy's son, Max, as a toddler, had used to express fear.

Ross said it back, "Scared!"

We watched Ted's boat go through. We could hear faint screams and see water splashing high into the air, but it was so far away, it was hard to grasp the magnitude of it. They made it through, and now it was our turn.

Tyler started up the motor, and we began our approach. We could see big waves clapping against one another in the churn, and as we got closer, the boat sloped up and down, more and more as the waves grew in size.

"IF IT FEELS LIKE YOU'RE UNDERWATER," Tyler shouted, "YOU PROBABLY ARE! HANG ON TIGHT AND DON'T LET GO!"

I tried to yell out a cuss word, but my lungs were in lock-down.

The boat went up in the air over a huge wave, and then dropped down so far we hit the surface at what felt like a perpendicular angle. We had nowhere to go but *through* the next wave, not on top of it. SMACK! It was exactly as Tyler had said: we were underwater, but not for long. The air in our raft caused it to pop out of the water at such a speed that all our bodies flapped about like flags in the wind. Then right back down again. CLAP! More water, and then up once again! WHOOSH! I gripped so tightly I'm surprised I didn't burn the flesh right off my hands. SPLASH! One more smaller wave hit before we settled out past the rapid.

Everyone screamed and laughed and high-fived and wooed, but I was frozen. Tears streamed down my face, and my hands shook uncontrollably. The tremors came not from the cold, but from the adrenaline rushing through me. I started to hyperventilate.

"Heeee-hoooo heeeee-hoooo holllly shiiiiiit." My breath was high-pitched and my teeth chattered.

"BoBo! Are you okay?" Ross asked.

"I'm okay! Just—heeeee-hoooo heeeee-hooooo—a little shaaaken!"

"Push it out!" Ross instructed, motioning with her hand to push my breath straight away from my body. She'd had panic attacks in the past and could see what was happening to me.

"Hoooooo." She blew out of her mouth and kept making the motion with her hand, "Push it out!"

I pushed my breath out and we both started laughing. We celebrated, water dripping down our faces. Everyone on the boat was giddy.

"That was *insane*!" someone declared.

It *was* insane. But I was okay. Maybe it was the peaking euphoria of an adrenaline dump, but just for a moment, cheering with my sister in that boat, trembling with delight, pushing my breath out, I realized I'd done it. I *hung on*. And I thought, *I guess it's all gonna be okay.*

chapter

six

"It's all gonna be okay," Mom looked up at Dad from the kitchen table with a calm smile on her face, red coffee mug in her hand. He was shocked to see her this way. The night before, he had called a doctor to see if he needed to get her to the emergency room. She had been catatonic, almost unable to speak.

Three days earlier, he had confessed.

During those three days, the phone didn't stop ringing, and I walked through the house on tiptoes, hoping to catch whispers of what might happen next. I found myself listening for the sound of approaching sirens, convinced that at any moment a SWAT team would raid the house and take Dad away.

I was filled with questions, but I only asked two, and I asked them in the first few minutes of that family meeting.

"Do I still get to go to SEP?"

SEP was Summer Enrichment Program, a camp for dorks at the University of Virginia. Unlike normal summer camps, where you learn to capture the flag and roast marshmallows, at SEP you got to live in dorms and go to architecture classes and pretend you were a college student for two weeks. SEP was crucially important to me, because it was another chance to live like grown-up Cristy—but now it was in jeopardy, because I knew it cost money. According to my initial calculations, we would now have to redirect the SEP funds toward paying for tents to live in and canned meat to eat.

"Don't worry about that, I'm sure we can work it out," Mom said. She then calmly announced, "Everyone can stay home from school tomorrow, to spend time together as a family."

And this, *this*, I could not abide.

"NO! I will NOT stay home! I CAN'T stay home! I am in the SCHOOL PLAY!"

I had to explain to these peasants that, at Midlothian

Middle School, the rules *clearly state* that you are not allowed to do after-school activities if you call in "sick." I realized that we were in the middle of a massive family crisis, but as Viking #3 in a musical adaptation of the famous comic strip *Hägar the Horrible*, I was the bedrock of an entire theatrical production.

"You can miss one play rehearsal," Cristy assured me.

"The play is opening in THREE days!" I screamed. This was crunch time, not "take a day off to spiral with your family" time!

I threw my hands into the air, and asked my second question:

"WHY DO YOU ALWAYS TELL US BAD NEWS RIGHT BEFORE THE SCHOOL PLAY?"

(This theory made total sense. Years earlier, when I was in the second grade, my step-grandpa died the week of our school's production of *The Wizard of Oz*, in which I played another significant role: one of the Buttercup Girls, an entirely made-up guild of Munchkins with flowers for heads.)

I ran upstairs to my bedroom and slammed the door, knowing deep down that these fat tears had nothing to do with drama club and everything to do with what my dad had just told us. While the rest of my family sat downstairs deciding what to do with their "day off" (I guessed it would be a combination of crying and staring at the wall), I chose to focus on my art. I sat on my twin bed, opened up my tattered photocopy of the *Hagar* script, and studied my one line:

"CHARGE!"

Mom did not have a script to follow. She shut down, her body stiff in the cold shock of the truth. She had no job; it had been years since she'd worked; she had done everything for Dad; she'd stayed home for him, played this role for him. What was going through her head? Did she wonder if it was somehow her fault? Did she think about leaving him? What options did she have? She did not ask these things out loud. She appeared frozen.

That Friday, during Dad's desperate phone call, the doctor told him to keep a close eye on her, and if she hadn't improved, to bring her in on Monday. Dad barely slept, terrified of the unknowns he had unleashed. The next morning, he came downstairs, and there she was, sitting at the table, acting completely normal—in fact, she looked better than she had in years.

"I talked to God last night," she said, "And He told me it's all going to be okay."

During their chat, God and Mom came to the conclusion that not only would this be a turning point, it would be one they'd navigate together. She would stand by Dad, she would forgive him, she would take responsibility for her part in it. She was all in.

"I had become so full of pride with all of my worldly possessions," she later wrote, "that a taste of what I thought was the good life had made me greedy. I wanted more and more, and it was never enough. Billy and I hit rock bottom. God really had my attention now! We called out to Christ."

(Dad describes it differently. "When she said it was going to be okay, I just decided to let go and hold on for dear life, no matter what came next.")

Later that day, my parents went to see Mike, the youth pastor at our church. Mike was not your stereotypical youth pastor—he didn't rock a ponytail, or wear a cool chain wallet. Mike was balding, sang baroque hymns with a classical guitar, and was super into wolves. You might think he wouldn't mesh well with teens, but he had a radical quality to him—a friend once described him as "more a Buddhist monk than Baptist minister." He welcomed my parents into his office with open arms.

During the meeting, the decision was made to surrender everything to God. They felt that part of the surrendering would require a public reckoning, a humble request to this church—a community they'd only been peripherally involved with—for forgiveness and for help. They decided to get up in front of the congregation the next day and tell the truth.

I do not remember this event. Neither does Jay. Neither does Ross. Neither does Cristy.

Each of us blocked it out, even though we all know it happened. My parents had stood in front of hundreds of people, some of whom were my close friends, and had wept openly, admitting to living a lie. As much as I wanted my parents to get on the same gold-trimmed page of the Bible as me and get right with the Lord, at that age, I also preferred everyone thinking that I didn't even *have* parents. Winfree had become my haven from worry, awkwardness, and embarrassment; here, the uncool were made cool. It was the one place I felt like I could just be me. And now Mom and Dad were up there, blowing it all up. It was not something I ever wanted to think about again, so my brain took the liberty of erasing it for me.

I *do* remember feeling confused in the days after, because even though Mom and Dad broadcast their secrets to the entire congregation, at home, the message to us was different.

"It's best if we don't discuss this with other people," Dad said. "This is a private family matter. And if someone calls the house when we're not here, do not tell them anything."

I took this guidance very seriously, worried that if I said the wrong thing to the wrong person, I could make things worse. Strange adults *were* calling the house, and I would stumble as I delivered my practiced speech of "He's not home. May I please take a message?" One time a man with a deep voice followed up with "Well, do you know where he is?" I hung up in a panic.

A week later, at school, I heard a mocking voice ring out across Mr. Hockenberry's third period class.

"I heard Sara Schaefer's dad is a THIEF!" some kid yelled. I was shocked. How did he know?

I pretended to not hear him. I looked down, opened my binder, and rubbed my hands on the fresh loose-leaf, hoping the coolness of the page would make my face less red. I thought if I was just still enough, that somehow the sound of his donkey bray would suspend and dissolve in midair. But the entire class had turned to look at me. I wanted to scream back at the kid, and at all of their judging faces, but nothing came. I was muted by my own lack of information. I didn't know how to defend my Dad because I wasn't even sure of what he had done.

("We sent letters to all your friends' parents," Mom told me fifteen years later. "We knew there might be rumors, and we wanted them to explain to their kids what was going on. We did what we thought was right.")

In addition to the letter, my parents took all of us to see a therapist. As we arranged ourselves in his office, I felt as if I were going to barf all over the floor. The idea that we *needed a therapist* just underscored that this was all very very bad and we were, as a family, in very very big trouble.

The therapist looked like Woody Allen. I will be honest, I didn't even really know who Woody Allen was at the time, but I actually remember thinking, *This guy looks like Woody Allen.*

Woody Therapist talked to us in soft tones that made my skin crawl.

"I know that things are really tough right now," he cooed.

Oh no, here they come, I thought, my eyes stinging. *Tears.*

"It's okay to cry," Woody Therapist said, detecting my tears on his feelings radar.

"I'm not crying," I croaked, "I have allergies." It was so obvious I was lying, but I just didn't want anyone to think I was having a hard time with this. In fact, I was *happy* this was happening!

Which was not a lie—part of me *was* happy. I was happy because even standing there in the still-smoldering rubble of our old life, I could already, tangibly, recognize a near-instant change for the better. Once the initial shock of Dad's confession wore off, it was clear a course had been corrected. My dad was already a different person. Bad Bill was nowhere to be found. His once-clenched jaw was now chewing gum. His once-icy eyes were now sky-blue optimistic. The pep in his step made me want to skip. The air was cleaner all around us.

Woody Therapist pretended to buy my lie about the allergies and continued.

"Let me tell you a story. Once there was a little boy . . ."

He proceeded to tell us a story about a boy whose dad played in a basketball tournament. It was the championship, and the score was tied in the last few seconds of the game. The little boy's father took a shot as the clock hit zero, and the ball bounced off the rim. The boy was so ashamed and disappointed in his father. Woody Therapist paused for dramatic effect.

"And do you know who that little boy was?"

Even though I was still a kid, I knew damn well who that little boy was.

"It was *me*," he said, as if dropping the mic. He waited for our minds to be blown.

The room was dead silent. I wondered if this story sounded right to Cristy and Jay, because they were older and definitely above such childish allegories. I wanted to ask them, *Did he really just compare losing a basketball game to what's going on with Dad?* But we all just stared at the floor.

We never went back.

By summer, we had sold the house, the Porsches, and the potpourri. During an estate sale, strangers ambled around our house and plucked things away one by one. Our status as a wealthy young family in Midlothian disappeared. Mom and Dad lost friends and endured gossip. Her siblings were furious, and for some time they tried to keep our grandma away from Mom and the rest of us. We moved from Salisbury to a less prestigious neighborhood where the houses were smaller and closer together.

Inside of me, the story got smaller and closer together as I memorized an easily digestible version of what had happened. Dad became his own cautionary tale. He had made a lot of bad choices. Then, he had made a crucially good one by telling the truth. Mom forgave. Jesus forgave. We forgave. The end.

But lying in bed at night, I kept thinking of a Bible verse from Mark: "Whatever is hidden away will be brought out into the open, and whatever is covered up will be uncovered." *Soooooooo true.* Dad tried to hide his secret, but even *I* could tell something was up! There's no use in trying to cover up your bad deeds! In fact, it's best to just avoid doing them in the first place! I swore to myself that I would never repeat his mistakes, and the lesson set permanently inside me like a bone healing out of place.

In the afternoons, I rode my bike around our new neighborhood with a much-needed new friend. Her name was Rebecca, and she was dorky like me. During this time in American history, a new obsession had taken hold of teen girls: the Best Friend Necklace Set from Claire's. It came with two necklaces, each with a pendant of a heart cut in half. The two jagged pieces of the heart fit together perfectly to reveal the phrase "Best Friends Forever." Splitting a BFF necklace meant that you were tolerable enough to have at least two friends, among whom you have been ranked the best. It was not an *OFF* necklace (Only Friend Forever Necklace), it was a *BFF* necklace. I didn't know where I stood in the social strata anymore, so I desperately wanted this badge of normalcy. All I had to do was lock a bitch down. As the BFF necklace craze swept the school, the pickings were getting slim.

Thankfully, Rebecca was still available, and I was picking up very strong BFF vibes from her. I worked up the courage to pop the question one day at school. I planned on proposing next to her locker, but as I approached her in the hallway, I saw it: a silver chain around her neck. Dangling from it was that unmistakable tiny half heart, glinting in the fluorescent light. I was too late.

I was stunned. At my locker, I dipped my head almost all the way inside, pretending to be looking for something, so that I could let a few tears out in private. The bell rang, I composed myself, and went to third period. There, I opened my notebook and set pen to paper. I wrote Rebecca an epic two-page proclamation, listing all the reasons why no, actually, *I* was her best friend, and that she had made a grave mistake. I may have also added a sentence along the lines of "Whatever. I didn't want to be your BFF anyway. You SUCK." (I definitely did.)

I folded the pages into a neat triangle, dropped it on her desk on the way out of class, and walked away in slow motion as the entire world burned down behind me.

That afternoon, as I rummaged around in the kitchen for a snack, the phone rang. Jay answered it.

"Sara, it's for you."

I picked it up, expecting to hear the voice of a teen girl, hopefully one of the few remaining loner girls without a BFF necklace.

"Hello?" I said.

"Sara Schaefer?" It was the voice of a strange adult, but instead of looking for Dad, she wanted me.

She continued, "This is Mrs. Simmons, Rebecca's mom."

I froze.

"Rebecca is *very* upset. I read your note. How DARE you speak to my daughter that way!"

"I . . . I . . ." I was already crying. *Whatever is hidden away will be brought out into the open, and whatever is covered up will be uncovered.*

"Do you want me to tell your parents what you've done? Do you? DO YOU?"

There was no Swunty in her voice; she had gone full cunty. To make matters worse, Rebecca's father was the *chief of police*. At a time when I was legitimately worried that a team of officers was going to burst into our home and drag my father away, I had angered the daughter and the wife of the *chief of police*!

I was in a free fall of terror. I slid down the wall with the phone to my ear, and through choking sobs, I begged this adult woman for mercy (who I now know was definitely one of the people who got that letter from my parents, so she knew exactly what she was doing).

"Please. PLEASE! I just . . . my FEELINGS were . . . I'm sorry!" I cried.

"Well then," she said, "you can write an apology letter to Rebecca and I won't tell them."

She hung up and I sat there, heaving.

That night, under the covers and by flashlight, I wrote the note. In it, I pleaded with Rebecca not to show the note to her mom.

The next afternoon, the phone rang again. It was Rebecca's mom.

"NO," she said. "This apology was NOT acceptable!" I don't remember at all what her beef was with my note, but whatever I wrote (I was twelve) wasn't up to this bitch's snuff. She threatened me again and demanded I write another note.

The next one must have satisfied her, because I never heard from her again. In the wake of it all, I shakily accepted that I had flown too close to the BFF sun. I gave up on the idea of splitting a necklace with anyone, and made a vow never to speak of this incident. (Until many years later, when I told Mom, who said, "What?! I wish you had told me. I would have destroyed that woman.")

School felt perilous. There were too many unspoken social rules, too many surprise humiliations, too many spies for the chief of police. Church was more manageable. At church, no adults bullied me and Jesus was my BFF. After all, I had a necklace with him already—the cross my parents gave me on Christmas.

I started a new diary, titled *The Spiritual Journal of Sara Schaefer*, and addressed all my entries directly to God himself.

> *Dear God,*
>
> *Who knew? Christian books are better than normal! I mean, some people think that if you're going to be a Christian, you have to give up a lot. Not true—you can get everything (just about) in the "Christian" version. (Music, books, habits, friends, etc.) I like Ben Keefer. He's such a sweet babe. But Ben doesn't like me. . . . You know, I take*

that back. Ben may be a babe but certainly not

sweet . . . more like a JERK! I think I like Jeff Mapp.

Well, I've got to be going now! I LOVE JESUS!

(Now <u>there's</u> a sweet babe!)

I know it sounds like I was all horny for Jesus (and maybe I was), but this was also me trying to be funny. I already had an inherent sense of irony, and every time I wrote in my diary, I was consciously trying to make Future Me laugh.

The leads in the school play were going to prettier, less awkward girls. I would always get the funny role, like an angry German camp counselor named Helga, or a pig named Roseanne who rants about acid rain. "Comedy is harder," my drama teacher told me once. I understood she meant it to be a compliment, but playing an old woman while your nickname is already "Grandma," or a pig when you are already getting called ugly, doesn't exactly inspire Eric Wilborn to come up to you at the winter dance to ask if you would like to slow dance with him to "Tears in Heaven," an incredibly romantic song that, at the time, we did not know referred to Eric Clapton's four-year-old son falling fifty-three stories to his death.

Still, part of me knew my drama teacher was right, and the ability to make people laugh felt like wizardry, like divine power, or maybe just like I had control over something.

Meanwhile, Mom tried to grasp her own sense of control and attempted to rejoin the workforce. Her nursing skills were outdated, so options were very limited. She found a job changing soiled bedsheets at a shoddy convalescent home that looked like it was, at any moment, about to get exposed for elder abuse by a local news problem-solvers segment.

As for Dad, he resigned from the Bar and lost his career. And that SWAT team? Never came. When Dad approached all the concerned parties with the truth, they agreed to let him try to make things right. It might have been luck, or privilege, or some combination of the two, but one thing was clear: the fact that he had come forward, before anyone even suspected something was off, made a huge difference. He asked for forgiveness, and it was given. The phone calls from strange adults dwindled. One of Dad's remaining friends gave him a low-level job, and we began the long road back to okay.

chapter

seven

I knew it would only be a matter of time before I got The Question about what I did for a living. We had set up camp for the first night, and now everyone was gathering around the kitchen while the guides cooked. New friendships were being established, some with the help of alcohol. (Ross and I had decided to skip the alcohol on this trip.)

As everyone loosened up, I met a Brooklyn couple named Andrew and Erin, who were on an epic road trip to all the major national parks before moving to Minnesota. There was a loud-talking guy named Dan, and his wife,

Shelly, whose hair and makeup still looked great. I wondered how her beauty routine would hold up down here.

Dan was already talking shit.

"Did you see those people?" He was referring to the family of four. "Didn't help unload the boat at all." It was true—when we first came ashore, the four of them had rushed to nab the best campsite and lingered there while the rest of us did the heavy lifting. The father, dressed in head-to-toe yellow-and-black spandex, had brought an inordinate amount of expensive photography equipment, and the wife had already changed into flowing linen pants as if she were ready for cocktail hour on a cruise ship.

The other person who stood out that first night was Bob. He was leathery tan and had the voice of a full ashtray.

"My family warned me not to drink on this trip," Bob said, jovially, while sipping a beer. "They say I'm a Jekyll and Hyde!"

Before I could worry too much about how that might play out, someone asked me The Question.

"What do you do?"

There it is, I thought. I briefly considered lying. Sometimes while traveling, I will lie about my occupation—not because I don't enjoy talking about my life with other people; I'm a comedian after all, which means I *love* talking about myself. But sometimes I lie because the very fact that I am a comedian means that if you truthfully answer The Question, the response is *always* one of the following:

"That's so cool! Can you tell me a joke?"

"Say something funny!"

"Well, you're going to get a *lot* of material around here!"

"Are you gonna write a joke about me?"

"I love comedy. You know who I think is funny? [Insert name of comedian who isn't funny.]"

"You know, people always tell me I'm funny. I could totally do it."

But here, in the Grand Canyon, with just my sister and twenty intimate strangers, I knew that lying was not an option.

"I'm a comedian."

"Oh wow!" she said. "I've never met a comedian! Honey! She's a comedian!" It practically echoed off the canyon walls.

Her husband's eyebrows arched. "Oh? Neat! You're going to get a *lot* of material on this trip!"

"Yes!" I said, "I'm sure I will!" Word spread around the camp pretty quickly, and I got each of The Comments at least once, especially the one in which the person requests a performance.

"This really isn't the setting for such a thing," I explained. "It's my job! I'm on vacation. Besides, my jokes aren't appropriate for children." *Thank God there are children here*, I thought.

The sun had just dipped down behind the cliff tops, and the orange glow on everything was magical. I was ravenous, and gobbled down several helpings of grilled salmon, rice, and salad made by our guides. As it got dark, everyone retreated to their tents.

On the Colorado River, the campsites have names like Badger and Hot Na Na and Lower Tuna and are mostly patches of sandy beach between the water and the cliff face. Some are tiny sand dunes, others are large thickets of seep-willow shrubs, desert broom, and wait-a-bit trees. I had figured that the sites would be reserved months in advance by our rafting company.

"Campgrounds in the canyon are first come, first served," Ted had announced earlier in the day. "Sometimes we'll have a ton of space for everyone to spread out, and sometimes we will be crowded together on a tiny beach."

After arriving at Sticky Beach, our first camp, Tyler gave a quick lesson on how to set up our tents and cots. I was overwhelmed by the number of poles and strings and flaps.

"See? Pretty easy," Tyler said, with the tone of a ten-year-old who just solved a Rubik's Cube in thirty seconds.

I knew it would not be easy at all, and I also knew that setting up a tent would be the first test of Ross's and my relationship. Would this be a trip where we bickered constantly, like we did as children? Or would this be a strengthening of our sisterly bonds? Everyone knows that assembling a tent with another human being is the single biggest threat to a relationship.

We calmly tackled the pile of silver poles and slippery waterproof fabric.

"No, wait. You hold the thingy," I said.

"What thingy? I can't see . . ." Ross said, irritation in her voice.

We were working with items that could not have weighed more than eight ounces each, but we were sweating profusely trying to get them to all come together in the shape of a tent.

"Hang on, dammit." A pole almost poked my eye out.

"Just tell me what to do," Ross said. We both knew we were one wrong move or testy comment away from becoming entangled in both the tent parts and a shouting match, but eventually we had a tent. Now all that was left was a search for "almost too heavy to lift" rocks to put inside the corners of the tent. Tyler had explained that winds whipped through the canyon without notice—not only could your tent blow away, but it could blow away *with you inside of it*.

Boulders in place, Ross and I stood sweaty and breathless observing our house for the night. It looked cozy. She went to grab some water to cool down, and when she got back, she said, "Oh my god, Sara, that spandex family."

I knew by the tone of her voice that she had some hot gossip.

"The wife. She's sobbing. The tent poles are everywhere. I get the sense that he did not fully explain to her how much we'd be roughing it."

I felt relieved that someone else in the group was less cut out for this than I was. But I also felt bad for her, because, man, fuck tents.

It had been a lot of work for something that we had been told we would barely even use. The guides said that sleeping inside the tents was most likely not a good idea, because they are essentially saunas in this heat. The only reason for the tent, they said, was if it started raining in the middle of the night. *The only reason?* I thought. *I can think of plenty of other reasons. Like, say, keeping bats out of your hair, or preventing a rattlesnake from giving you a nonconsensual neck massage while you sleep.*

Even though we were scared, Ross and I decided we wanted to follow the advice and attempt to sleep outside.

"I want to at least *try* everything on this trip," Ross declared as we tackled setting up our cots. "Even if I'm scared. I want to say yes to it all."

"Yes, I love that," I said. Her words opened a little door in my brain, one I hadn't known was there. I knew this trip would involve being *forced* to conquer some fears. But what if

I approached it from a place of choice? *It's all about choices*, I smiled to myself. What if I actively said *yes* to every moment? Maybe we would fail. But at least we could say we tried.

Back at the kitchen, Ted gathered us around and said, "It's time to learn about The Groover." He showed us a little hand-washing station set up at the opening of a pathway that went into the trees.

"This is the key to The Groover," he said, holding up a small plastic container of butt wipes. "Take it with you. If it's missing when you get here, that means the bathroom is occupied."

Next, we followed Ted on a little path around a bend to a small clearing that faced the river. There it was: The Groover, a humble metal tank with a toilet seat set on top of it.

"The Groover got its name," Ted said, wistfully, "because before we started using this luxurious seat on top, you just had to sit on the tank directly, and that would cause you to get a groove in your butt cheeks."

The Groover came complete with toilet paper, disinfectant spray, and the most incredible view of the Colorado River tumbling through the Grand Canyon.

"Nice view, huh? Just hope nobody floats by while you're doing your thing!" He laughed as we turned back to camp.

For nighttime pee breaks, we were given small blue

buckets. The horror of trying to wade into a raging river in the middle of the night hadn't even occurred to me. I was relieved someone had figured out that it was a really bad idea.

In the dark, our campsite did not seem cozy at all. It felt totally exposed. I had never slept *outside* outside before. Not having walls as a barrier—even thin fabric walls—terrified me. It was Ross who had expressed fear about this from the start, but I was now really feeling the vastness of everything myself.

"Ross, I'm so scared. What if I can't sleep?" I said.

"You can be next to the tent." She offered to create a cushion between the wilderness and me, so that I might feel the tent wall and her own cot on the other side of me as a type of fortressing. *Dammit. I'm already failing on my gremlin duty. She's the one who is more scared of the animals, not me!*

After a little while, someone came by with a purple light.

"Hey, would you mind checking around our campsite?" Ross said, her voice high—she had recognized it as a black light used for spotting scorpions.

With the scorpion check completed, we laid down on our cots. I got inside my sleeping bag, hoping it would create an additional feeling of security, but it was way too hot. I didn't want to sleep on top of it, because I wanted to be able to quickly get inside of it in case of a lizard attack. But I also didn't want the top half of it flopped over the side of the cot and touching the sand, creating a tarantula on-ramp, so I just lay there, totally out in the open.

"Oh my god, Sara, we are sleeping in the Grand Canyon! This is crazy," Ross whispered. This refocused me. By now, my eyes had adjusted. The stars in the sky twinkled, more than I thought possible. There was a blue glow coming from behind the canyon rim, making it easy to see, that yes, we were indeed inside the Grand Canyon. Somehow, this comforted me, and I started to feel protected by the canyon itself. I *was* inside of something. Something stronger than any structure made by a human.

I closed my eyes. The sound of the rushing river canceled out all the other sounds. I thanked the universe for this moment, made peace with my demons, and finally became one with nature. I fell into a deep, soul-restoring sleep.

Just kidding—I tossed and turned and cussed for six hours straight. Our campsite, which we had originally thought was perfect, was actually a nightmare, because it was set on a slight slope. Because the outside of my sleeping bag was silky, the entire thing kept sliding down the cot with me on top of it, and every thirty minutes or so, half my legs would be hanging off the bottom. Once I was readjusted, I would gradually start to drift off to sleep again, until WOOOOOSH! The sound of a wave startled me awake. In my twilight sleep, I thought it was the entire Colorado River about to wash over me. Or THWACK! Sometimes water would slap the bank, and I'd jolt awake thinking rocks were about to fall on my head. And the moon—my god, the moon! It was like a spotlight; so bright you didn't need a flashlight. I thought about sitting up and reading a book. That would have been a better use of my time.

Instead, I lay there, picking at every little thing in my head. *Ugh, selfish. You made Ross sleep on the outside. Bad.*

Everybody on this trip knows I'm a comedian now. Pressure's on. Better be funny tomorrow.

I don't feel funny anymore.

Finally, the heat gave way to cooler temperatures and sheer exhaustion put me under. About ninety minutes later, I awoke to clanking and banging noises floating up from the kitchen. I opened my eyes to discover that yes, I was actually still there, in this wild place, and it was even more beautiful than the day before. I sat up on my cot and looked around. The tip-tops of the cliffs were burning ember red in the dawn, and the air smelled like a combination of that distinct river scent and desert sage and morning dew. Even though I had barely slept, how could this scene make me feel anything other than the refreshment of a thousand day spas?

People started stirring in the camp, and Ross sat up. She looked around and saw it, too. She smiled at me.

"We definitely need to get a flat campsite next time," I said.

"Yes. Yes we do." She laughed.

Back on the river, I felt as if I were finally ready for some clarity. Now that the initial shock of the first day had worn off, I was ready to be reborn. I waited for the life-changing revelations to come.

I feel nothing, I thought, staring at the most beautiful congruence of marble and limestone—Bright Angel Shale, a layer just now breaching the surface, a half-billion years old, a sure sign we are going deeper, farther, getting older. Surely this is symbolic of something. *It used to come so easy. Just get up and make everybody laugh. Maybe I just don't have what it takes.*

I imagined my very funny friend Rory having the entire boat in stitches with his hilarious quips about the color of the river. *A real comedian is just naturally funny. You're just a poseur.*

I shook my head, trying to clear my mind of these thoughts. I couldn't believe I was down here in this amazing environment, comparing myself to a comedian in a completely made-up scenario and just *deciding* I had lost the competition! Why was I even thinking about my career at all? I thought you were supposed to go to raw nature to escape all that.

"Long ago, ancient tribes used to have tigers," Tyler said, mercifully interrupting my spiral. "They would allow their tigers to fight each other, in a symbolic ritual to avoid war and maintain peace. Afterward, the losing tribe would bring their injured tiger down to the river and wash it clean, right here. That is how this rapid got its name. Tiger Wash. Two-hand hold, everybody, two-hand hold. Tiger Wash."

We held on and hollered through the jaunty Class VI Tiger Wash rapid. After I emerged, spitting brown water out of my mouth, I started to wonder about the Tiger Wash story. I think it hit us all at the same moment, because just as I was about to open my mouth, someone else called out, "Where did they get the tigers?"

Tyler shrugged his shoulders and smiled wide.

"You just made that shit up, didn't you!" I exclaimed. Everyone started laughing. I realized that we had all blindly placed our trust in the guides.

"River Daddy," I whispered in Ross's ear. "That's Tyler's nickname. River Daddy." Not only was Tyler a handsome bear of a man, he was, functionally speaking, our father for the next week.

"It's perfect." She giggled and passed it on to the others. The nickname stuck, and pretty soon everyone was openly calling him River Daddy.

River Daddy was my first real joke of the trip, and it was

a success, but it wasn't long before the negative thoughts crept back in. *Oh of course you would feel proud of something like that. Jesus, Sara, can't you not desperately need validation for one second?*

I was getting so frustrated with myself. I couldn't have any feeling at all without judging it.

After setting up camp, we hiked to a place where four tiny square windows were carved into the rock face. These were the Nankoweap Granaries, where the Anasazi people stored food around 1100 AD. As we climbed toward them, a late afternoon thunderstorm approached. Even though Matt had assured us that lightning rarely strikes *inside* the canyon, it turns out that it's really hard to shake a lifetime of being told that you are definitely going to die if you are standing out in the open during a lightning storm.

BOOM! Thunder echoed through the canyon.

"Okay, that's terrifying," I panted as we climbed. The storm was getting closer, the hike steeper, and the raindrops fatter. I imagined the descent in a downpour. My ankle nearly twisted itself at the thought of going down what would essentially be a slippery stone staircase. I decided to turn back. As I faced down, I was startled by how high I'd climbed and had to lean against a boulder to steady myself.

The view was the most spectacular thing I'd ever seen in my life. Here, the Grand Canyon stayed relatively straight, and I could see the river snaking miles into the distance, the thunderstorm moving in, and the curtains of rain filtering the light in a way that would make Thomas Kinkade jizz his pants.

As I took it all in, I realized this was, aside from a visit to The Groover, my first time by myself on the trip. I suddenly spotted a distinct white dot on the hill much farther below me. I knew immediately that it was Ross, and I could just barely make out that she was trying to take a picture. I chuckled at how small she appeared, just a speck for scale.

There is something about seeing a tiny dot of a person I love from far away. I know the shape of you, even from a great distance. You are almost nothing in the landscape, but you are everything to me. I started to laugh, but the giggle jammed in my throat and started to convert to weeping. It was all just too much, and I thought, *Here it comes, here comes the breakthrough.* But then, CRACK! Another lightning bolt spidered across the sky and set me scrambling down the hillside.

Whatever epiphany this place was going to bring me would have to wait.

chapter

eight

It was the first holiday season after Dad's lightning bolt to our life, and Christmas morning loomed heavily. Mom kept saying depressing things to Ross and me in an attempt to prepare us for a big letdown.

"Christmas isn't going to be the same this year," Mom warned, her voice sullen.

"It's okay, Mom! We don't care about that stuff!" Ross and I reassured her. I did not want her to think I expected so much. Did she think we hadn't been paying attention? Because, uh, I *got* the message. Greed is bad!

On Christmas morning, we gathered at the top of the stairs as per tradition. Cristy and Jay rolled their eyes as Mom forced us to take a picture. This year, we didn't scramble down the stairs like racehorses—instead, we marched down in an orderly fashion, bracing for the disappointment we'd been warned about. We filed into the den, and to my surprise, there they were: four mini-mountains of presents! Sure, it was clearly less than years past, but Mom worked hard to make it *feel* like a lot. She boxed up things individually to increase the quantity. She re-gifted some items she had lying around the house, just to add height to each stack. Ross, Cristy, and I even got some nice jewelry.

"Mom, this is too much," Cristy said, worried.

"We weren't able to sell some of my old pieces, so they let us trade," Mom said.

Mom worked with what she had to make this morning special. But there was also a thin desperation in the air that no amount of wrapping paper could cover. I felt sad and embarrassed that she went to all this trouble to hide the fact that we were struggling.

Things got worse. Shortly after Christmas, Mom's mother, our Grandma, died, and shortly after that, her closest sister got news that her cancer had returned. A woman going through so much in such a short time might have collapsed. But Mom somehow started flying.

First, she threw herself completely into church life. Once a drive-by parishioner, she now couldn't make it out of the parking lot after worship service without at least an hour of socializing, organizing, and on-the-spot prayer sessions. She was electrified.

Dad was going to church, too; though, for him, the initial euphoria of his great unburdening was beginning to wear off, and sometimes his moods would return to darkness. Mom was constantly encouraging him to get out of his head and participate in church activities, one of which was a mission trip to New York City with Jay and the older kids from our youth group. When Dad and Jay returned, she was transfixed by their stories of serving in soup kitchens and helping strangers.

"I saw something today," Mom told us excitedly one Friday night in March over Chinese takeout. Gone were the days of her cooking onions in the pan. Now, we ate foods that required minimal labor: microwavable dinners, salad bar salads, frozen lasagnas, and the occasional takeout.

"I saw some men living under a bridge, so I pulled over and talked to them," she said, as if this were completely normal. She asked the men how they got by. They told her that weekends were tough, because all the soup kitchens were closed.

"I am going to take them some food tomorrow," Mom

declared. Sure enough, the next day, she and Jay made ten bagged lunches and drove them over to the men.

"I think we should do this every Saturday!" she said that night.

From then on, every week, Mom turned our kitchen into an assembly line of brown bags, and the entire house smelled like bologna. She and Jay would drive around and deliver the food to all the homeless encampments they could find. Eventually that spread to housing projects. Pretty soon it was too much driving, so she set up a couple of distribution points. She convinced our local Food Lion to donate day-old bread and donuts. And then she incorporated as a non-profit and called it Pennies For Heaven.

To help deliver the goods, Mom acquired a cargo van, complete with the Pennies For Heaven logo emblazoned on the side of it. The license plate read: PENNIES. It was creepy and smelled weird, so us kids nicknamed it the Kidnap Wagon. As the operation grew, Mom had to enlist more and more help. She got everybody at Winfree involved, and then she launched a far-reaching recruitment campaign by delivering presentations at churches and civic groups all over central Virginia. The presentation included a slide show set to music, including the seminal guilt-trip ballad of the 1980s: Phil Collins's "Another Day in Paradise."

As our garage filled with more and more bags of supplies

and donations, Mom dreamed bigger. By July, she signed the lease for a retail space downtown. The building sat on a part of Broad Street that was once a bustling shopping hub for upper-class Richmonders. Now the block was strewn with pawnshops and boarded-up buildings, but Mom decided this would be the perfect place for her Pennies hub. A thrift shop, food pantry, meeting place, and beacon. She commissioned a huge sign for the outside that read: THE MELTING POT: PENNIES FOR HEAVEN. But everyone ended up just simply calling it The Store. The Store's customers were a mix of local characters, bargain hunters, hipster students from nearby Virginia Commonwealth University, and people from the weekend program looking for some additional help. It was just like a regular store, except, among our racks of clothing, someone would occasionally take a shit on the floor.

"It ain't the mall!" Mom would say.

A home for mentally ill people sat right around the corner from The Store. A guy named Robert became a regular. He'd stomp in, slam a bunch of change on the counter, and angrily mutter, "Woman! Gimme a pocketbook!" After some struggle to get his meaning, Mom realized that Robert wanted a wallet. He'd purchase his pocketbook, march out of the store in a huff, and then immediately throw it into the trash can out front. He did this almost weekly. We were teens, so we'd laugh at this bizarre cycle and call him Psycho, but Mom wasn't having it. She would yell, "His name is *Robert*! He is a human being and he is *sick*. He can't help it!"

She loved Robert. One time she found out he was having surgery, so she took a huge bouquet of balloons to his hospital room. The nurses said she was the only person who came to visit him.

Mom was literally on a mission.

The mission was often all-consuming, which meant that when Jay, Ross, and I weren't working at The Store, we were frequently left to our own devices. More than once she forgot to pick us up from after-school activities and we'd have to walk the two miles back home. And now that she was done cooking meals every night, there was never much food in the house. She'd leave us a blank check for Papa John's if she was off doing her thing, but sometimes she'd forget, and we had to pay with whatever loose change we could find around the house.

Mom's attention was, for the first time in my life, focused on something outside of our home. In my diary, I complained about feeling like a speck of dust that no one noticed and even included pie charts illustrating how Mom's attention was divvied up (I drew my sliver of the pie melodramatically thin and labeled it "about 2%").

I made up for this lack of Mom's gaze by making myself visible in all other areas: school plays, church skits, home-

made movies with our gigantic VHS camcorder, piano recit-
als, raising my hand in class as if my life depended on it. Pie
charts aside, I wasn't angry at Mom. I yearned to be close to
her. To be like her. Her goodness was inspiring, the antidote
to everything bad that had come before.

I recorded my intentions to follow Mom's footsteps in
The Spiritual Journal of Sara Schaefer. "Dear God," I wrote, "I
made a decision. I want to serve you, Lord. I want my career
to be something that is oriented in the Christian field—
money does not matter to me."

By November, Mom was busy organizing something
she'd named "Distribution Day." In conversations with her
clients, she realized that the impending winter months
would be especially difficult for them. They needed new
coats, boots, sleeping bags, and socks. She called on the community to collect the supplies and arranged for special
touches like a machine to serve fresh hot popcorn to everyone who came. She even created a voucher system to make
sure everyone got what they needed. The first Distribution
Day was a huge success.

Weeks later, her sister lost her life to cancer. But Mom
kept going.

Every week there was a new idea. She collected Christmas stockings for children across the city's housing develop-
ments, and she was already scheming about next year's

Distribution Day. It felt as though we'd achieved some kind of momentum now, a current of purpose running through everything we did.

That Christmas Eve, Mom happened to look out a window and see that someone had pulled into our driveway and was unloading stuff—a bunch of rusty wire coat hangers and a broken children's bicycle, also known as garbage—from a minivan. Mom's body sprung like an angry cat.

She yelled, "UH UH . . . I DON'T THINK SO!" and stomped down to the gravel driveway. It was on.

The lady immediately got indignant. "I'm making a donation," she said in American Swunty.

"No," Mom said firmly. "Take it back." Not only were these items not on the list of acceptable donations, but Mom always told people to call ahead of time, arrange a pickup, or drop it off directly to The Store downtown.

"Well, SOMEbody could use it!" the woman replied.

Uh oh. (We had already learned that you *never* say that to Billie Schaefer. "SOMEbody could use this!" is a terrible way to think about your trash. The basic rule of thumb for donating to any type of charity like Goodwill is: if *you* wouldn't touch it, let your kid play with it, or wear it on your body, then SOMEbody doesn't want it, even if it's free.)

Mom wouldn't back down. "No! Take it back! It's Christmas Eve! I have a LIFE!"

After a short standoff, the lady repacked her car and drove away. Mom came inside, slammed the door, and proclaimed, "Some people just do NOT get it!"

We laughed. We got it.

Within a few years, this was our new normal. The Schaefers of the past seemed like strangers to me now. Mom's mission wasn't a phase; this was who she was. She never stopped thinking of new ways to help people.

One day, she said, "What if Harold lived with us for a little while?"

Harold was a wiry blond man whom Mom had met at the lunch program. He was relatively young and strong and offered to help with deliveries and odd jobs around The Store. She paid him what she could, but he had nowhere to live, so she let him sleep at The Store sometimes. That soon felt insufficient in her mind, and now that Jay was off at college, we had the extra room. She invited Harold to live with us on a temporary basis.

Luckily, Harold was nice and funny, and not a pedophile. This was a huge relief, because not only was he crashing in a house with teen girls, but part of his job was also to regularly drive a vehicle nicknamed the Kidnap Wagon around town. He'd joke, "Hey Billie, I think there's something wrong with the van. It shimmies when you go over ninety." He made really good chicken fingers from scratch, and it started to feel a little normal to have him around. But one day, Harold wrote himself a sizable check from the Pennies checkbook and disappeared. We never saw him again. Mom's theory was that Harold was on the run and that his name probably wasn't Harold. She'd recently asked him about his social security number, which had come back invalid after she'd filed taxes, and that must have spooked him.

Mom dealt with all kinds of disappointments and betrayals at the hands of people she was just trying to help. But Harold hit her particularly hard. He really was like family. She understood that he may have felt he had no other choice, but she did not understand why he wouldn't at least leave a note explaining himself. She was sad, but not surprised. She knew the risk of opening your door to people who were down and out. She knew that sometimes you were going to cross paths with people who'd take advantage of your kindness, or people who had bigger problems than you could ever hope to alleviate. Everyone has a story behind their bad choices. She knew this all too well.

I tried to absorb this attitude into my own heart. By now, I was flying right alongside Mom. I attended a geeky magnet school called the Governor's School for Government and International Studies. I was a leader in the youth group at Winfree and I sang in the youth choir. I even participated in *extracurricular* church shit, with a nondenominational fellowship called Chrysalis, which was the teen department of a Christian community called Emmaus.

I stuck to the straight and narrow. I never tasted alcohol or tried drugs, and sometimes to my own detriment. Even though all of my friends were either classmates from my nerd school or fellow members of church groups, most of them were standard issue teens. Everybody I knew did something naughty, whether it was drinking or touching one anothers' privates or even jaywalking. And I never engaged in any of it, even if it meant feeling humiliated or alienated. At one party, my classmates played spin the bottle. I literally *left the room* because I did not want to be forced to French kiss or *worse*. I could not be peer-pressured. I was made of stone.

But when Mom asked me if I would be willing to lend my guitar to a homeless couple, I struggled.

"Just for a little while. They are musicians and they can play music on the street to make money," she said.

My guitar was my prized possession; it was my passport to cool. I regularly practiced Indigo Girls songs on it and fantasized about luring cute boys with my siren music. Hadn't I done enough to help? But then it occurred to me that this was a "shirt off your back" moment, the kind we always talked about at church. Jesus gave his *life* so that I could lend my guitar. The couple was so grateful. I felt like a hero.

Then they disappeared the next day and I never saw that guitar again.

At The Store, thievery was commonplace. Break-ins happened more than once, and Mom would often catch people shoplifting. But she had no fear—she'd walk right up to the perpetrator and scold them, waiting with her hand out for them to pull out whatever it was, usually a cartoonishly square item poorly hidden under a T-shirt. I don't know how she had this power, but they would almost never run and would instead relinquish the item. Then she'd say, "Now get out of here and don't you EVER come back! You hear me? If I see your face again I'll call the police!" If they showed up again—and she would never forget a face—she'd shout, "UH UH! No sir! Go on! I told you!"

Still, Jay took it upon himself to beef up security. He and Mom somehow acquired a Taser, and he created a homemade mace by hammering a bunch of nails into the business end of a baseball bat. Neither ever got used.

I can only remember my mom calling the cops a few times. Once, she discovered a sandwich baggie of cocaine in one of her storage unit hauls (beyond donations, Mom found stuff to sell at The Store by bidding on abandoned storage units—long before the show *Storage Wars* made it trendy). She called the police station, expecting the DEA to swarm within minutes. But whoever answered was unimpressed and told her to just flush it down the toilet.

"Hmph! Well, what good are they?" She shrugged with a laugh.

Another time, somebody robbed Pennies at gunpoint. Mom's friend and employee, Boo, was working the register while Mom sat up in her office on a little balcony overlooking the showroom. Boo—already an exceptionally calm person—coolly handed over the money in the cash register, which amounted to about forty dollars. Mom ducked down behind her desk and called 911 as quietly as she could. As Boo told it, the robber saw the forty dollars and pushed the gun forward into his chest.

"Where do you keep the *big* money?"

Unfazed, Boo said, "Sir, we are a non-profit charity. This IS the big money."

Both Mom and Dad worked themselves to exhaustion trying to make ends meet. Early on, they tried to earn extra money selling skin care products from a company called Nu Skin, which was famous for its glacial mud masks. Ross and I really enjoyed slathering the thick goopy dirt all over our faces and experiencing the sensation of it slowly drying and cracking over time. You had to scrub like hell to get it off, which I'm guessing is what actually gave you that subcutaneous glow, not the magical Icelandic minerals the products claimed to contain. Eventually, we abandoned Nu Skin, because it wasn't all it was cracked up to be.

Instead, Mom and Dad picked up a second job at an unlikely place: Winfree. The church posted a job opening for a janitor, and they inquired about it, asking if it would be okay if they split the duties. And by split, they didn't mean two ways; they meant four to six ways, depending on if Jay and Cristy were home or not. This was going to be a joint Schaefer effort. Every weeknight we headed to Winfree and formed a custodial Voltron to complete the work of one janitor in under two hours.

Some nights I was on trash can duty, other nights I got stuck with toilets. Dad did the bulk of the work and was always in charge of vacuuming, because he had a lifelong obsession with clean floors. (We still make fun of his "Finger Sweep"— he cannot make it two feet through the house without leaning down to pick up some microscopic piece of dirt that only he can see.) No matter what the assignment, we completed it as quickly as we possibly could, practically running through the building so that we could be done and get dinner. We were all so busy with everything else in our lives, the very last thing any of us wanted to be doing at the end of the day was scrubbing dried apple juice and urine off the Winfree preschool bathroom floors. We often bickered throughout the process.

"Sara got to do trash last time!" Ross would complain.

"No, I did not! You always do trash! I always have to do TOILETS!" I barked back.

"GIRLS! Quit it! Oh Jesus, help me. I am about to have a nervous BREAKDOWN!" Mom would say.

Every night upon arrival, Mom would give a pep talk. "Okay. It'll go quickly if we all work together. Please, Jesus, don't let there be a big ole mess in there." The job was back-breaking work already, even without a Big Gulp spill in the choir room or a shredded-lettuce explosion from some kind of sandwiches-and-prayer meeting. Whenever we encountered a surprise mess, Mom would cry out, "Oh good GRIEF! Who do these people think they are? Lord, HELP me!"

Dad was still along for the ride. He was in lockstep with Mom, but sometimes money stress and her wild ideas left him weary. Even though Mom was humbly saving the world (she now had set her sights on global causes—she even volunteered at a refugee camp on the edge of Rwanda *during the genocide*), she also had no qualms about the spotlight it shone upon her. She never hesitated to show off her good deeds to the local media or up in the pulpit of some church. She was a natural up there, and she knew her enthusiasm would be contagious. But I could tell that living in her shadow made Dad feel like the tiny speck of dust that no one could see. What piece of the attention pie was he getting?

And so, occasionally, Bad Bill would reappear, and I couldn't stand him. Bad Bill was really hard on everyone around him. He scolded and punished me for the smallest infractions. Granted, I could be annoying—I put so much pressure on myself to be good at everything, and I would get easily overwhelmed and scattered. I would freak out over extra credit assignments and constantly misplace important things. One time, I left a lasagna cooking in the oven for two hours too long and ruined dinner. It came out looking like a black slab of volcanic rock.

At such times, "Dad" would throw out his "it's all about choices" line, but if "Bad Bill" were on the scene, he would snarl and say things like "Sara, for someone so smart, you can be pretty damn stupid."

I was incensed when he came down on me, because I felt like I was owed the same grace we had all given him. I hated when he passed judgment on me, or anyone for that matter.

How dare he? We forgave him.

chapter

nine

The weather on day three was unforgiving. We covered a lot of miles on the river, huddled together on the boat in head-to-toe rain gear, getting pelted by glass-like shards of hail. Even a tiny splash of water was a frigid bitch-slap, and people started taking turns riding in the front in cold sacrifice. I was still too scared to sit up there, and for this, I passed judgment on myself.

Selfish. Bad Sara.

I also had a migraine. It felt like a knife was going through my eye and out the back of my skull.

The campground at Trinity Creek that night was small, and somehow Ross and I landed on the beach last, so the only spot we could find was right next to the kitchen. Before the trip, Ross's friend had recommended we find campsites away from the noise and smells of cooking food, so we felt discouraged. But as we set up and got comfortable, we realized that it was the perfect spot for us. It was closer to the rafts, where the guides slept and could more easily hear our cries in the event of a bat swarm, and it was less distance for us to drag our equipment. As it turned out, not being able to take the heat meant staying as close as possible to the kitchen.

At this campground, the cliff walls stood closer, and even post-rainstorm and post-sunset, they radiated heat. When Ross tagged along for the nightly scorpion hunt, she discovered that anyone sleeping against those rocks was surrounded by the tiny beasts, and she called me over to look. The scorpions' bodies glowed purple.

I was dead tired and my gums were throbbing from the migraine. Because it was a little cooler, Ross and I decided to try sleeping inside the tent, and the stillness it provided put me down almost instantly. Hours later, Ross woke me up with frantic whispering.

"Sara. Sara! What is that noise?"

I listened. It definitely sounded like something alive, a

squeaking. Our tent was nestled under a tree, so I figured it was a winged creature.

"It's just birds I think," I said, and rolled over to go back to sleep. Ross wasn't convinced. She sat up and unzipped the front flap of the tent.

"Oh my god! Sara!" she gasped. "It's those little furry things they were telling us about! What are they called?"

I shot up on my cot and grabbed my headlamp. "Oh my god, ring-tailed cats?" I said.

"YES!" We both hurried out of the tent to try to get a glimpse.

There they were, three or four little balls of fur running all around the moonlit camp.

So far on the trip, we'd seen all kinds of wildlife: desert bighorn sheep, great blue herons, even a collared lizard. But the ring-tailed cat was the one I really wanted to see, in part because they do not look like they belong in North America. Their eight-ball eyes bulging out of their tiny heads and their bushy striped tails make them seem exotic, like the type of animal you'd only see at the zoo or on a Nat Geo show about Madagascar. But here they were, right in front of us, playfully digging through the recycling bag, jumping up on the kitchen worktables, and loudly chatting with each other while their tails quivered with delight.

We tried to keep quiet, but it was hard to contain our excitement.

"They're so precious!" Ross squealed.

"Hello, my little buddies!" I whispered.

I checked the time: 4:45 a.m. Our wildlife moment had the blood pumping, so we decided to stay awake. I realized my migraine was gone and felt a surge of energy and positivity. Being woken up by the cutest animals in the Grand Canyon had me feeling like Snow White. Today was going to be a good day.

After breakfast, we packed up the rafts and took our seats. I noticed that, over on the other boat, the dad from the family of four was still wearing, on this, the fourth day, the same head-to-toe, skintight yellow-and-black spandex. I declared henceforth that he should be known as "Spandad." Everyone on my boat agreed.

By now, Spandad was getting on all of our nerves, because day after day when we made it to our campsite for the night, he and his family would abandon ship, swipe the best spot, and not help unload. ("IF YOU'RE NOT GOING TO HELP," Dan had shouted one evening, "THEN I'M NOT UNLOADING YOUR HEAVY-ASS CAMERA EQUIPMENT!" I don't think Spandad heard him, because he was down the beach tending to his angry wife.)

Ted made an announcement.

"Today we've got a lot of big water, including Crystal Rapid," he said. "It's our first ten, and it's the most consequential rapid on the river. Pay attention, hold on tight, and let's have some fun!"

Consequential? I did not know what that meant but it sounded ominous.

Before I could worry too much about Crystal Rapid, right off the bat we hit two IXs: Granite Rapid and Hermit Rapid. We thrashed our way through the rough waters, screaming and laughing all the way. On smaller rapids, some people started riding the outer tube of the boat like a bull, hanging on with one arm like they were at a rodeo.

As we approached Crystal Rapid, we pulled over to the bank to make final preparations. The guides messed around with our boat's motor, stopping and starting it a few times. I appreciated the precautions, but my stomach lurched thinking that this next rapid was so big it required them.

Back in the current, River Daddy gave us his usual rundown. This time, it was not a homespun tale. Instead, he had cold hard facts.

"Crystal Rapid was formed overnight," he said seriously. "This used to be relatively flat, until a debris flow in 1966 pushed a bunch of boulders into the river. We're going to navigate through the curve to the left and avoid the rocks in the middle."

Everyone prepared, locked down their water bottles, and got into position: Two-hand holds, facing forward, total quiet. Once again, the waves grew and grew, and we tipped up and down. I knew by now that when the boat tipped upward toward the sky, we were in for a huge crash on the other side. Right before we went up, I heard River Daddy say, "Oh my god."

It was happening way too fast for me to turn and scream, "Wait, *you* are scared???" The wall of water hit us hard, and up again we went, getting smacked with waves over and over. The boat seemed totally out of control, and the boulders in the middle of the river seemed to be pulling us in. Tyler was revving the engine, and it sounded as if he were in a battle against the currents. I figured this was just what navigating a X felt and sounded like. Crystal finally spit us out on the other side into calmer waters, and we all cheered. I was shaking this time, but not as badly as before. *We did it!*

"The engine died," Matt said flatly.

I gulped. *Wait, what?*

"But we're fine!" River Daddy brushed it off, though I could tell he was a little rattled. "Crystal Rapid is no joke. If we had gotten stuck on those rocks, we would have had to stay out there in the middle until the Park Service could come rescue us."

"So like what, a couple of hours?" I asked.

"No, like one or two days. We'd all have to sleep on the boat out there. You get real close to the other people on the boat. Real quick."

Then, it hit me. That word *consequential.* What they actually meant was deadly.

I was surprised that our temporary engine failure did not paralyze me with worse fear than what I brought with me into the canyon. Instead, it boosted my mood. *Now we're having an adventure. I'm an epic stunt beast. I eat life-threatening situations for breakfast, bro.*

Instead of negative thoughts, now I was coming up with funny ideas.

"What if there was a river guide that wouldn't stop bringing up his personal problems?" I asked Ross, and then did a voice kind of like River Daddy's.

"Comin' up, bit of a bump. This one's called Granite Rapid, and it's pretty savage, kind of like my ex-wife. She won't return my calls. . . . Granite Rapid!"

We kept laughing thinking of the various things that the Oversharing River Guide might slip into conversation.

"Next up! Tanner Rapid. They say this rapid is named after a nineteenth-century prospector, but I like to think it's named after the bastard who stole my wife. Hang on tight to the raft . . . and to your woman. Tanner Rapid!"

Not only was my mindset changing, so was the scenery.

Tapeats Sandstone was everywhere now, the last letter in our "Know The Canyon's History, Study Rocks Made By Time" device. Tapeats Sandstone looks like matzo crackers stacked up, a lighter beige with uneven, singed edges. And lately, just at the river's edge, the relatively level lines of the layers were being met with a new, diagonal section of rock, pushing jaggedly into it at an angle.

"This is the Supergroup," said Matt. "You can see that it's diagonal. Above it is a line called the Great Unconformity, a mysterious billion-year gap in the rock record, between the Tapeats Sandstone and the metamorphic rock beneath."

I watched as we passed a never-ending variation of stone, sometimes gleaming marble, and at other times red-streaked, like some ancient megabeast had bled out on a plateau above. Then, River Daddy turned off the engine (this time on purpose). Everyone got quiet. The walls of the canyon were forming an echo chamber, a soundstage of impeccable acoustics. I took a deep breath, ready to hear the whispers of the universe.

But then, instead I heard the sounds of a heavily choruspedaled electric guitar in E minor.

It was coming from the back of the boat, through a speaker of some kind. I recognized it immediately. It was "Nothing Else Matters" by Metallica. I looked back and saw River Daddy smiling knowingly.

Everyone burst out laughing. We had to sing along, it

was just too ridiculous. We belted out those metal lyrics like moody teens and let our angst ricochet through the canyon. But then our giggles died down, and the power of the moment hit. Truly, nothing else mattered.

———————

Before stopping for the night, we made a side hike into a slot canyon at Royal Arch Creek.

"How deep are we now?" I asked.

"About a mile down," Matt answered.

A clear mile from the rim, I felt so far away from the world. My worries finally seemed to be up there, not down here.

"How old is this wall?" I asked as I steadied myself against it.

"This is the oldest rock in the Grand Canyon," he said. "The Elves Chasm Gneiss. It is 1.8 billion years old."

It was hard to grasp the idea that what I was looking at was almost two billion years old. I felt so insignificant, my life's little dramas so fleeting. The rocks were so permanent, so immovable, yet also somehow in constant motion, almost fluid under my hand as I dragged it along the stone curves. *Has any human ever touched this spot? Or what about this one? Am I the first? Does my touch help shape this place? Surely it is shaping me.*

As we hiked farther in, the hiking became more difficult. The fourth guide, Jesse—basically a gecko who could skitter up any wall barefoot—helped me maneuver around a small outcropping of rock, teaching me some basic rock-climbing techniques.

"This is FUCKED!" I screamed, feeling totally vulnerable as I hugged the boulder for dear life.

"You got it, now, put your foot here." Jesse pointed to a tiny ledge that looked like it could maybe fit a small gathering of ants.

"WHAT THE SHIT!" I followed his instructions and placed my toe on the ant balcony. He held out his hand for me to grab. On safe ground, I pumped my fist into the air.

"I can rock climb now!" I shouted, like I was ready to attempt El Capitan without ropes.

"I wish you could have seen what I saw," Jesse laughed. "You were up there acting like you were gonna die, but you were only two feet off the ground."

We arrived to our destination: a cascading waterfall splashing down some fifty feet into a pale aqua pool. A rainbow sprang from the misty spray. We waded into the exotic-looking swimming hole and then climbed up and along dangerously mossy rocks inside the cave to get to a ledge inside the waterfall.

"Jesus, you are a wizard," Ross said, quoting the daredevil

Nik Wallenda, who walked a tightrope across the Grand Canyon 1,500 feet in the air without a safety net. During the stunt, he was miked and could be heard talking to Jesus throughout, repeatedly referring to him as a wizard and commanding the rope to calm down.

"In the name of Jesus, I command these rocks to calm down!" I said back.

After our waterfall experience, I splashed around in the water below. I was starting to get chilly, so I waded out to warm myself in the sun.

"Your high beams are on," Bob joked. I was confused at first, until I saw him nod his head toward my chest. I looked down, and sure enough, my nipples were hard as Kaibab. I forced out an uncomfortable chuckle.

"Yep, thanks for the heads-up, Bob," and I quickly grabbed my towel to cover up.

"Gross!" Ross said after I quietly told her what had just happened.

"I guess we're starting to find out what that Mr. Hyde is like," I said as I took a swig from my water bottle.

———————

"Wooooow," Ross and I said in unison as we pulled up to our campsite for the night. Big Dune is a huge sandy beach set against a palatial expanse of Tapeats Sandstone. No vegetation, just sand and rock and a panoramic view of the river. Other than a hot wind whipping sand in our faces, it was perfect.

After bathing in the river (a process that involves washing your entire body and hair, while still clothed, as fast as you possibly can, and then throwing yourself violently underwater for a bloodcurdling rinse), I lounged in my dry camp dress, happy on the beach. I looked around as various members of the group washed up and took photos. The tween girls used sticks to draw pictures in the mud on the river's edge. Shelly shook out a towel. Somehow, her hair and makeup had defied science and was still perfectly intact. Before long, a few others pulled up their camping chairs next to mine.

"I can't imagine what doing stand-up comedy would be like. Is it a tough thing?" someone said.

By now I felt more comfortable talking about my career.

"Yeah, it's a weird life," I said. "In social settings, being a comedian has kinda spoiled my ability to be normal. My job is to be funny, so when I'm around a new group of people, it feels like work to be funny. But then I come off as way too serious, and people are left wondering if I'm funny at all. And then I start feeling the need to be funny, because, let's be honest, it is the only thing that makes me feel alive! Hahaha, anyway, I think I'm broken!"

He stared at me blankly.

A little later, Ross and I hung around the kitchen as the guides cooked dinner.

I had taken a liking to Jesse, who had a thick Southern accent and a weird sense of humor. His nickname, he told us, was "Earthworm," but when I asked him how he got that nickname, he smiled impishly and shrugged his shoulders.

"So, are you like, famous?" Earthworm asked.

"Absolutely not," I said. I turned to the snack table to grab some crackers. I could hear Ross talking low behind me.

"Yes, she kind of is," Ross said. "She won't admit it. But she's done a lot of big stuff. She's very successful."

I wanted to turn and disagree, because, at best, I am only "famous" in extremely niche situations, but overhearing Ross's bragging warmed my blood. Her pride in me was obvious. Sometimes it's just nice to have a hype man around to toot your horn for you. I pretended to not hear it and rejoined them.

The idea of performing for the group came up again. I once more resisted, but then, River Daddy had an idea.

"What if we do a no-talent show on the last night of camp?"

"What's a no-talent show?" I asked.

"People just get up and do whatever. That way you can perform, and it's not a big deal."

"That's perfect!" Ross said.

I wasn't sure it was perfect.

After the sun set, everyone created a circle of chairs and socialized.

"Oh my god, look!" Andrew shouted and pointed up at the stacked cliffs behind us.

A glowing lantern had appeared on a ledge fifteen feet above us. (In lieu of campfires, which were banned in the canyon, the guides had been making a nightly lantern out of a tin can, cloth wick, and lighter fluid.) I could see Ted scampering farther along the small cliff. He was setting up lanterns all along the sandstone.

"It's magic!" Ross yelled. The entire beach lit up in the flickering glow, and the shadows danced on the stones. Ted's creativity must have been contagious, because suddenly, inspiration hit.

"Maybe I'll write a song about the trip for the no-talent show," I told Ross. "It's a way to perform for everybody without having to tell my jokes."

I retreated to my cot. As soon as I lay down, it felt like a hair dryer was blowing directly on my face and someone had poured sand into it. Big Dune was beautiful, but there was no plant life to protect us from the howling canyon winds.

I created a shield with my sheet and stared up at the glowing Tapeats sandstone. I wondered if I would be able to pull off the song idea. A minute ago I was excited about it, but now it had me feeling squirmy.

I've performed in some high-pressure situations. Huge theaters filled with thousands of people who have no idea who I am. The comedy tent at a music festival, every sound drowned out by a literal rave going on next door, to hundreds of people who have no idea who I am. Live television, from the old *TRL* studio in Times Square, beaming into hundreds of thousands of homes filled with people who have no idea who I am. College gigs, in cafeterias, filled with three mouth-breathing freshmen who have no idea who I am. I know pressure. So why did I feel so much pressure to do this tiny, nothing performance? The stakes could not have been lower, but it felt like I had everything riding on it.

t e n

"It's going to be okay," Mom said. "I promise you. You are way too hard on yourself, Sara."

Her voice on the phone had already started to calm me down.

"Now," said Mom, "when you hang up the phone, I want you to take a deep breath. And then I want you to go get yourself a Diet Coke—with a LOT of ice. And then I want you to take a shower. Promise me?"

Mom's solution to almost any problem was to go get a Diet Coke with a LOT of ice and/or to take a hot shower.

"Okay, I promise." I hung up the phone, took a deep breath, and grabbed a can of Diet Dr Pepper (close enough) from my mini-fridge. Then I did that thing that always helps when you have thirty-two deadlines and not a minute to spare: I lay on my dorm room bed, stared out the window, and let the slow paralysis of anxiety take hold.

And about an hour later, I heard a knock at the door.

———

When I started college, I'd been dreaming of going for the better part of six years, ever since my nerd camp, SEP, had given me a taste. I would be attending the College of William & Mary, which sounds like a fancy private school, but is actually a state school that I could afford to pay for by myself through student loans. As excited as I was for this new chapter, I was also freaking out about it. I was a little concerned about my faith. On campus, the devil would surely be afoot, and I worried about not fitting in. Would any of these strangers relate to my simultaneous appreciation of the hipster-Christian teachings of Jars of Clay *and* the period-blood moon howlings of Tori Amos?

But these were trifles compared to a much larger looming fear.

Thumb. Yeah, remember Thumb? I was suckin' it this *entire* time. I had become a master concealer of my habit, but I knew college might leave me exposed. Thumb was so intrinsically a part of my existence that I wouldn't even realize I was doing it, and this fact implanted a terror in me so deep I barely slept during the weeks leading up to freshman orientation.

For this reason, it was vital that I showed up on the first day looking fly. Makeover sequences in film and TV have taught women to subconsciously expect that their entire lives can change with the right haircut. So, the day before move-in, I excitedly sat down in a salon chair and specifically requested "a minor trim with long layers." A radical choice. The "stylist" nodded and prepared her scissors for transformation.

Have you ever pranked your hair "stylist"? Like, when they make that first cut, you scream and pretend they made a horrible mistake? It's fun, you should try it. What's not fun is when you actually scream because they are actually making a horrible mistake. The woman had cut a chunk two inches above my eyebrows, which, if you factor in my curl, resulted in a half-inch lock of hair boinging perpendicularly off my face.

This monster had given me a bang.

"WHAT ARE YOU DOING?" The entire salon of yappy suburban ladies fell silent.

The "stylist" said, "I'm . . . cutting your bangs. I was just doing what you told me to do."

If I had actually died right then, which is what I felt like doing, my final words would have been a quivering whisper: "long . . . layers . . . long . . . lay—[the light leaves my eyes and I go to Jesus]."

A different "stylist" came over and trimmed the rest of my hair in suffocating silence. I think she was so scared to do the wrong thing with my new bangs that she just kind of stopped in that area and left them glaringly uneven. When it was over, I paid the fifteen dollars I owed them and walked dead-eyed out of the salon. I now had a slanted forehead. Every single person in that Fantastic Sams knew I looked hideous, and don't you dare claim otherwise.

I got into the car and drove home screaming. This was NOT how I had intended on beginning my new life. As I pulled in to the driveway, Mom was driving out in the Kidnap Wagon. She rolled down the window, a huge smile on her face.

"Let me see your hair!!"

I shrieked from my car window to hers, "AWFUL!" I could barely get the words out through the sobs. "RUINED!"

She stopped the van and got out, and I could tell from her reaction that I wasn't imagining the destruction.

"It's not that bad!" she said. "Can we go back and get it fixed?"

"NO! Unless you're going to GLUE BACK MY OLD HAIR then NO!" I don't know why I refused to have someone even out those bangs. Maybe I thought it would look worse if the short sprigs went all the way across. Or maybe I wanted everyone to know about the injustice that had been done to me.

The next day, I arrived at William & Mary on an insanely humid August day in Williamsburg, which is about an hour and fifteen minutes east of Midlothian. I waited in line for my orientation packet, feeling my hair nightmare grow increasingly worse in the tidewater heat. I pushed my chest out to try to give my cross necklace maximum visibility, hoping that some like-minded Christian would come over and pray for my hair with me.

On that first night, I climbed into bed and waited to hear my roommate's sleep-breaths, and then turned my body toward the wall, pulled the covers over my head, and practically sucked the skin off my thumb. But things quickly got easier—no one seemed to care about my hair. In fact, it made for a good story to break the ice, and almost immediately, I homed in on a subset of girls on my hall who seemed to like laughing about it as much as I did: Annabelle, Amy, Gianna, Mellie, Jill, and Emily. These girls, according to my checklist, definitely belonged to the Bad Girl Club. They drank alcohol, had sex, smoked clove cigarettes, and puffed weed through a toilet paper roll. We'd gather in Gianna and Amy's room and listen to Belle and

Sebastian songs and talk through the whole totality of human existence.

We also delighted in the new frontier of the internet. That year, Dupont became the first-ever dorm at William & Mary to get hooked up. As the first class to gain access to one of the most significant inventions in human history, we harnessed the power of the information superhighway to expand our knowledge and connect with the world. Just kidding—what we actually did was log on to AOL chat rooms and, as a group, pretended to be a singular horny woman, lure some sad man into having cyber sex with "her," and laugh our heads off as said sad man typed out his fantasies, presumably with one hand. It only occurs to me now that we may have been chatting with another group of giggling girls crowded around a different computer.

That said, if it *was* indeed a man, he probably would have jizzed out his entire insides if he'd known he was chatting with a team of barely legal coeds. I don't think the joke was on him.

Yet despite these newfound friends, I missed my family and was struggling to make sense of my separation from Ross. By the end of high school, I had gone from gremlin fighter to diplomat and adviser. Ross's cute childhood mischief had morphed into teenage drama, and the stakes felt much higher. I helped hide evidence, provided alibis, and frequently lobbied my parents to go easy on her if she stumbled in her studies or got into a fender bender. In turn, I'd try to shove her into the straight and narrow, pleading with her to see it from Mom and Dad's perspective. Though I felt noble in my peacemaking efforts, if I was being honest with myself, I often intervened in a bid for my own comfort, because I hated fighting. But now that I was gone, it didn't matter, because Ross had to fight her own battles while I was off focusing on myself. Whenever I tried to counsel her on the phone, it was clear I wasn't helping. I didn't know how to fix what was going on between her and Mom and Dad, and I actually feared that if I didn't somehow intervene effectively in her life, she'd run away from home and our entire family would fall apart. I too often hung up feeling as if I were failing her as a big sister.

Even though I was forging new bonds with the Bad Girls Club, I was still living in an iron maiden of my own rigid morals, abstaining from partying and touching junx (a term one of the Bad Girls, Amy, had coined to describe sex). It all made me lonely, and I felt torn between my old life and my new one, worrying that I was going to become bad. I was spending too much of my spare time in bed sucking Thumb. Someone must have told our RA, Liz, that I was too sad, because one day she knocked on my door.

"Hey, are you all right?" Liz was a Super Christian. Before I could answer, she was already kneeling.

"Can I pray for you?"

I trusted her completely in this moment. She was only one year older than me, but as an RA, she may as well have been one thousand years old. When she said "Amen," we lifted our heads and opened our eyes. In the expectant silence, I felt obligated to explain myself, as if she had consulted with the Committee of All Christians and they had determined I was backsliding into wickedness. I don't remember much of what I said, but I do remember that when she left the room, I felt even worse. I felt cornered and accused, even though she hadn't said jack. I still loved God, but my heart was changing. I balked every time I learned some new story about a religious institution harming those I thought we were tasked with loving. I was shocked to find out that Christandom was chock full of authoritarian thinking, homophobia, misogyny, and racism.

I stopped wearing my cross necklace. I'd become distinctly aware that it meant so many different things to people, and I didn't know how to answer for them all. Instead, I chose the Bad Girls. They were so free and they never chided me for being a goody-goody. They seemed more Christlike to me than the Super Christians lurking about, who seemed so *sure* they were the righteous ones.

What's more, the Bad Girls provided the perfect conditions for me to reveal my big secret. One night, we were sitting around and somebody suggested we take turns revealing embarrassing secrets to one another. Jill admitted to having one long nipple hair. A bunch of us howled "ME, TOO!!" The laughter made me bold. When it came to be my turn, I just spit it out.

"I still suck my thumb," I said. I waited for the record scratch and subsequent screams of horror and why-god-whys. But instead, two (two!) other girls just said, "Oh, me, too!" Somebody else said, "Who cares?"

Later that night, alone in my room, I Netscape Navigated the term "adult thumb-sucker." (Google wasn't a verb yet.) I hit the search button, and was immediately greeted with a rudimentary website called ThumbsuckingAdults .com, which begins with this simple paragraph:

> For all those years you thought you were the only
> person on the planet thumb-sucking at your age. Well,
> you finally found the right place! Forget the past and
> all those bad thoughts you've had about yourself (if
> you have; some don't, you know); here we can come
> together and share our feelings on this subject. Fact
> is, there are probably millions of adults thumb-sucking
> worldwide, mostly hiding their method of tension relief
> because of perceived and real social stigmas associated
> with this gentle habit. Here you will get to express your

thoughts and experiences about adult thumbsucking
and see that it's not as uncommon as you've believed.

My lungs ballooned with air I'd never breathed before. Finally, after all this time, a simple web page, full of information and FAQs and testimonials, was here to tell me I'd gotten the puzzle all wrong. *There is no sickness.* What I believed this whole time to be a catastrophic psychological defect was just a run-of-the-mill habit like biting your nails, or doing cocaine in a casino.

This was the first time I discovered that a story I had told myself about the world and my place in it was not true at all. It shook me down to the balls of my feet, and now all my perceptions were up for debate.

———

Unsheathed and ready to find out who I really was, I spent sophomore year searching for a purpose. I stepped naturally into the role of RA, which I enjoyed for the most part, except when I had to discipline people. By now the Bad Girls had taught me that their behaviors I initially perceived as dangerous and bad—having sex, gulping beer, getting a GPA slightly lower than 4.0—weren't bad at all. They were simply *normal.* But then there were the Rules, still beckoning me back to my comfort zone. I worried about pleasing my supervisor and the possibility of a young girl dying of a Natty Light overdose on my watch. I felt overwhelmed. I wondered, *Am I really cut out for being the boss of others? Can't I just be nineteen years old for a minute? And when am I going to finally touch junx?*

By the end of sophomore year, I had auditioned for twelve acting roles in college productions and was denied every time. I also got turned down by the campus improv group for a second year in a row, which for me was the kind of rejection that stays in the body forever, like LSD or herpes. When I called home sobbing to report the news, Dad asked Mom, "Sara's room is on the first floor, right?" He was half-joking, but half actually concerned that I might jump; that's how completely distraught I was. Even though nothing made me feel as good as I did when I could entertain a group of people, I couldn't ignore these red flags of rejection. Maybe I was not meant for a life of performing? And also, what does a penis feel like?

I still idolized Mom, so I decided that maybe a life of service was my calling. I signed up for a six-week summer volunteer program in Honduras. The people I met there, and the extreme poverty they survived, dismantled even more of my perceptions, and I came back to school newly aware of my sheer luck: I had been born a white, able-bodied Christian in one of the wealthiest nations on the planet. I was going to make it count. Failure meant failing the entire population of Honduras, and arguably, the world.

In my mind, the best way to succeed was to fill my schedule to the absolute brim with more and more activities and responsibilities. I returned to my RA position, and I was a member of William & Mary's first sketch comedy group (Finally! I got a yes!). I obtained a highly coveted role in the main stage production of *Much Ado About Nothing* (I was the stage manager), wrote a weekly column for our student newspaper, *The Flat Hat*, participated in something called the Women's Leadership Program (all I remember is the lady in charge teaching us how to properly wear a pantsuit), served as historian for the Theatre Student Association, and I helped Mom with the Pennies For Heaven newsletter. I was in a sorority, because what better way to spend my spare five seconds per semester than bedazzling sweatshirts while speaking in hushed Swunty tones about those bitches over at Kappa?

I also studied.

But I was barely keeping it all together. I kept misplacing vital items like keys, money, and IDs. During a particularly frantic episode of tearing my room apart trying to find a notebook, Jay told me over the phone, "Stop. Stop looking for it. Step back. Come back to it later when you are calm, and it will appear." I followed his advice, waited a day, and found the elusive notebook. These moments of wisdom were brief, however, and I mostly just felt as if I were in a free fall of missed deadlines and forgotten duties.

Ross and I were still clashing, and even things with Cristy were tense. During a weekend home, all of the women of the family were bickering over something stupid. Dad and Jay were nowhere to be found, most likely because, at the first sign of trouble, they went into "Operation Scatter," a term Jay invented to describe anytime two people start arguing and everyone else runs for the hills. This particular fight escalated when Ross threw out our relatively new nickname for Cristy: "PC," which stood for Perfect Child. (In the Schaefer wars for attention, we had determined that Mom thought Cristy was perfect. It had begun years earlier, after Cristy had gone to college. When we came down for breakfast on the first day of school that next year, Mom had placed a framed eight-by-ten of Cristy on the kitchen table where she usually sat, and we had to quietly eat breakfast with it. Afterward, the eight-by-ten was moved to the fireplace mantel, and gradually, Mom created a little altar to Cristy there, with multiple photos on display. Of course, Mom did this because she *missed* Cristy. Mom didn't need an altar for us, because we were right there sitting in the family room with her. And yes, Mom created elaborate altars for each of us once we moved away. But at the time we were shitty teens and did not understand.)

"STOP CALLING ME THAT!" Cristy screamed.

In group fights like this, it could get wild—Mom begging Jesus to help her, Ross threatening to physically fight anyone who dared come near her, Cristy stomping off into the wilds of our subdivision, me slamming doors.

I tried reasoning with Cristy.

"PC is just a joke! We love you! They call me PCIT and I don't get mad about it!" I said.

"What is PCIT?" she said, her blue eyes glistening.

"Perfect Child in Training!"

At this, she burst into bigger tears.

"Well, that's just not true. Because you think I'm a LOSER!" she said. This was new.

"What?" I said.

"Remember when you said, 'Now you can finally start your life'?"

I had to think about it, and then I recalled a conversation we had when Cristy announced to the family that she would be moving to Arizona with her boyfriend. I was pumped for her move and, without thinking, I exclaimed, "Now you can finally start your life!" Since graduating from UVA, she had been working in Charlottesville for a couple of years, and this adventure west seemed to me the next logical step toward the dream of being a bona fide adult. But now it seemed like her once-fawning little sister had been declaring her a sloppy loser with no life.

"Oh my God, Cristy, NO! I do NOT think you're a loser! MY FAVORITE COLOR IS ORANGE BECAUSE OF YOU!"

"Lord help me," Mom quietly prayed to the ceiling, adding, in the most pathetic voice possible, "They'll be sorry when I'm gone."

The family room was quiet for a moment, and then, we all burst out laughing.

"Mom, stop!" I said. The "You'll be sorry when I'm gone" comment had joined "Christmas isn't going to be the same this year" in Mom-isms that we regularly imitated. She knew it was funny and melodramatic, but she also knew it would end the fight, like a blanket smothering a fire.

Back at college, I felt like I was juggling grenades with the pins removed. One day, all of the pressures of college and family and global poverty and this quasi-adulthood I had so badly wanted all of my life came to a head when some girl with a pom-pom for a brain shamed me for not fulfilling all of my sorority duties. Over the phone, she had cheerfully told me to "Get *motivated*!" That's what sorority sisters are for, right? Inspirational quotes in a time of crisis. I hung up the phone and felt so much better.

Just kidding, I threw my phone against the wall and went berserk. I wailed and thrashed around on my bed, pounding the thin mattress. An avalanche of self-hatred flooded my brain. I couldn't find a breath.

I decided to call Mom. That's when she told me I was too hard on myself, and that I should get a Diet Coke—with a LOT of ice—and take a shower.

An hour and fifteen minutes later, there was that knock on the door.

It was Mom.

I couldn't believe she was standing there. She was holding a gigantic basket of snacks, stuffed animals, and various secondhand knickknacks she no doubt got from the shelves of The Store. I imagined her hanging up the phone with me, swiftly throwing things into a basket, and hopping into the Kidnap Wagon to come see me.

"I don't want you to be stressed," she said, handing me the basket. "Now, I don't have much time. I only have about an hour before I have to drive back to Richmond."

I knew how busy she was. She was just like me— overcommitted with her *own* thirty-two deadlines. She put that all aside, and for an hour, 100 percent of Mom's Attention Pie Chart was dedicated to me.

We walked on Colonial Williamsburg's cobblestone sidewalks to get lunch. Crunching on pickled okra, Mom said, "The thing about you, Sara, is that you've always got your goals. You've got your long-term goals, and your short-term goals. It might seem like too much now, but you'll get it figured out."

"I know," I said.

"'Get motivated'?" she said, referring to the pom-pom's comment. "I'll show her 'get motivated!'"

We daydreamed about the future. I told her I was going to write a book one day about The Store. We brainstormed titles and settled on *It Ain't the Mall*. It would make a million dollars, so I could buy her and Dad a country house, complete with a river for Dad to fish in.

And then it was time for Mom to go back. I walked her to the Kidnap Wagon.

"Bye. Talk to you soon," I said, my lip quivering as I turned away, not wanting her to see me cry.

She had been right, too—I had short-term goals (reducing stress levels, murdering a sorority sister) and long-term goals, though these were less clear. With the end of college just around the corner, all I knew is that I wanted to do something grand with my life. It was just a feeling, something I could not quite verbalize yet. Would I be a movie star? Would I return to Honduras and make a real difference there? Host a late-night talk show?

In my journal, I wrestled with my yearnings for stardom, which seemed to be in direct conflict with my sense of charitable duty:

> *I love to entertain people. I love to make people laugh, to make them smile, think, and become better people. Is this bad? I feel and experience things that I have this <u>dire</u> NEED to share in any way that I can. It's weird, but I want to be an entertainer. Am I narcissistic? Selfish? It sounds like I am about to declare my decision to enter the entertainment business—to be on TV, movies, whatever. Every inch of my desire says YES, do it, but there's that fear again: Sara, you don't have what it takes. Sara, you aren't good enough. Sara, it's selfish. Is it?*
>
> *Oh, and boys. What are they?*

I couldn't help myself. I knew Future Me would find that last line funny.

Future Me would soon find out what a boy was, because

at the end of junior year, I fell in love with one. *The* one. One and done. He was the funniest person I'd ever met. I felt like I had won the lottery, and I immediately decided we'd be together forever. I showed up to the relationship like an Army recruit reporting to boot camp: ready to surrender my possessions, my body, my whole self to the cause. I would die for this love if necessary.

I floated through senior year on a wave of enchantment. I took naps with him, tried beer for the first time with him. I touched junx with him. We had a secret language built from inside jokes, and together we daydreamed about conquering Hollywood. Maybe he would become a big-time movie director, and maybe I would become his star. He gave me permission to want those things. I was not a bad girl for drinking and having sex and wanting to be an entertainer; I was an in-love girl. A love so big it felt like God's love. It felt right and good. I could do all things through Boyfriend who strengthened me.

I graduated college, and with Boyfriend by my side, I was finally ready to start my life.

chapter

eleven

In Blacktail Canyon, the air is cool between the rocks. Ted had led us to a cavern there, a cathedral for our concert.

Everyone spread out, sitting on our life jackets; Ross and I tucked ourselves against the upward sloping walls. Ted and Jesse broke out their guitars and started playing. I looked up at the curvy ribbons of sandstone, climbing ever higher, the sunlight zigzagging down through the canyon's slim opening. At eye level, the light diffused into a gauzy glow. No one talked—it became a full hour of communal stillness. Some people lay down on smooth slabs, some began snoring.

At one point, I looked over to find Spandad dancing by himself. His gyrations looked exactly like the kind of movements someone with the nickname "Spandad" would think acceptable. He was both *in the pocket* and *really feeling himself.*

I panned my gaze farther back along the canyon trail. There, in the distance, I spotted Spandad's wife, leaning against a rock, sulking. I thought about offering to send a video of this moment to their marriage counselor, whom they would surely be hiring the very moment the trip ended.

"Does anyone else play?" Ted said.

"Sara does," Ross said, pushing my shoulder into the direction of the instruments.

"I am terrible," I said, not lying.

"Come on," Ross said, "You know you want to. I'll sing with you." She was right, I *did* want to.

"Okay fine," I said, taking the guitar. People perked up, as if they were about to see a secret tomb unearthed.

Ross knew exactly what song I was going to play. At Chrysalis—that extra-credit Christian group we had both joined in high school—our favorite song to sing had been a reworked version of "Amazing Grace," set to the tune of "Peaceful Easy Feeling" by the Eagles. After a few false starts, I got to strumming the chords and we began singing.

"Amazing grace, how sweet the sound . . . that saved a wretch like me . . ."

My hands started cramping up because I was so nervous. I tried to focus on the strumming and kept pushing the words out. Our voices bounced around the cavern.

I couldn't remember the words to the second verse— because honestly, who can?—so I abandoned the song.

"Whatever. You get the idea," I said.

Everyone clapped. Thankfully, when you're stuck a mile down into the Earth's crust, people's standards are really low when it comes to musical abilities.

"Play something else!" someone asked.

"I don't know many other songs," I said, starting to blush. *God you're so corny. Stop hogging the guitar and give it to someone who can actually play!*

I started trying to pick out the chords to Indigo Girls' "Closer to Fine," which I had played countless times as a teen.

"Are you trying to play 'Closer to Fine'?" Andrew asked.

"Yes, but I can't remember it exactly."

"I know it," he said. I practically threw the guitar to him. He started strumming those familiar chords.

Ross and I sang, just absolutely hitting the shit out of those harmonies, beaming with cliché. I kept laughing at how hokey it was, but then I started really listening to the lyrics as they came out of my mouth, and a sob rose in my throat.

Damn you, Indigo Girls! This is way too on the nose. It's

true! My whole life I've been stuck between black and white! Wrapped myself up in a blanket made of fear! I've been to a fucking doctor! I've been to the stupid mountains! I drank from many [airport] fountains! Shit. Maybe if I could stop needing everything to be so definitive . . . maybe I could get a little closer to feeling . . . fine!

We finished the song, and the group rejoiced.

Back on the boat, my heart soared, and a new thought appeared like a white flag on the battlefield of my mind:

What if it's okay to want to be heard? To be in the spotlight? What if my talents are a gift, and the selfish thing would be to hide them? I tried to let the question hang there for as long as possible until it blew away in the wind.

The cliff walls closed in around us. As our boat creeped through the narrowest part of the canyon, a spooky corridor called Granite Narrows, I felt as if I were entering a gateway into some ancient kingdom ruled by serpents. What was on the other side, we did not know, but we were traveling toward it, hoping for safe passage into this new place.

chapter

twelve

New York City would be the perfect place for my new plan: to become a comedian. With college done—and after a year in New Orleans while Boyfriend went to graduate school for film—I took a train from Richmond to Manhattan, just weeks after 9/11. When Mom and Dad had dropped me off at the station, the air had felt jammed with meaning.

"Here, take this," Mom said, pressing a one-hundred-dollar bill into my hand. "Don't spend it. Have it in your wallet at all times and use it *only* in an emergency." Though she and Dad were totally supportive, they were visibly

141

afraid of my choice to move to New York at this particular moment. The past few weeks I'd heard the same question from everyone in my life: "You're *still* going?" Planes were weapons now; anthrax was in the mail. Ground Zero was still smoldering, and I had lost an old friend in the North Tower.

But I was determined to stay the course. After New Orleans, I had decided to go for it. I figured that I should do it while I was still young. That way, if it turned me into an evil person, I would at least have time to remedy it, especially if I were a celebrity who could lend my face to telethons and the like. So, when Boyfriend decided he wanted to quit grad school and try novel writing, we hatched a plan with a friend from college to move to New York City. Caitlyn, a fellow member of our sketch comedy group at William & Mary, would pursue comedy with me, as a duo of sorts. She had a connection to a *Saturday Night Live* cast member, so this was going to be pretty simple: move to Brooklyn, take an improv class or two, achieve darling status, and both become famous comedians within a year.

I got a day job as a financial researcher for a law firm to pay the bills, but immediately trouble brewed with Caitlyn, who lived with Boyfriend and me. She questioned my commitment to our dreams, suggesting that my choice to work such a time-consuming job meant I was not serious about comedy.

She had chosen something more flexible and lightweight—walking dogs for her *SNL* contact. Why couldn't I have done something like that? Great question, Caitlyn.

"You're not going to believe what I found lying on the kitchen table," I whispered to Boyfriend as we lay in our bed one night. "A bank statement. She has a bunch of money! It's like a trust fund or something!" I was furious. I had moved to the Big Apple with just enough money for our rent deposit, an entire college education to retroactively pay for, plus one one-hundred-dollar bill that I had been explicitly instructed *not* to spend! Where had she gotten that safety net? And now she had the gall to shame my need for full-time employment?

Everything deteriorated, and within a year, Caitlyn moved out and we parted ways for good.

The law firm I worked for purported itself to be a team of white knights fighting fraudulent corporate giants, but the deeper I got into the work, the murkier this mission seemed. Profit was always the top goal, and we were going to slither through every loophole to get it. This isn't an indictment of this particular firm; in fact, I think they did a very good job for their clients. But in my moral rigidity, I would stew over any perceived ethical breach and huff at how hollow the entire operation seemed in comparison to *real* heroic work, like feeding the poor or making television. It didn't help that my boss, a walking yacht named Gary, would regularly fart during meetings and give me career advice like "you know, if you want to make it in comedy, you should wear short skirts when you perform." I spent my days eyeballs deep in spread-sheets and New Matters Reports, dreading Gary's name popping up on my desk phone. He would frequently call me into his office to make some impenetrable request, like "Is there a way to make this number bigger?" I would have to in-form him that, no, I did not know how to make $2 + 2 = 25$ million dollars, and this would anger him.

I spent every spare moment working on comedy ideas. On the train, I would scribble down thoughts in a spiral-bound notebook. So much of it was about Mom. Often-times I would just list funny things she had said, but had no idea what to do with them.

I had never tried comedy by myself. What would I say? Was it possible to do a sketch by myself? Caitlyn was gone. Boyfriend wanted to write novels by himself. Who would work with me? What about stand-up? I wouldn't need an-other person for that. How do you tell a joke? Where would I go to perform? Will the other comedians make fun of me? Though I was taking improv classes, I was desperate to find a way to perform on my own. I could get the guts up if I could just come up with something funny to say.

None of my ideas seemed good enough, and my cubicle

increasingly felt like a coffin. One particularly bleak day, my stapler ran out of staples, so I dragged myself to the office supply closet for a box of refills. The number on the box caught my eye: 5,000. Five thousand struck me as an absurd number of staples. I thought: *There's no way I'll be here long enough to go through this entire box.* So right there, in the dark clutter of a supply closet, I made a deal with myself: *You will be gone from this place before this box is gone. Within five thousand staples, my life will be different.* I took the box and nestled it in my desk drawer.

A few nights later, I was noodling on a Casio keyboard when suddenly, inspiration struck. I decided to write a moody ballad about my cubicle. I feverishly wrote it in less than an hour:

> When I'm with you
> Your walls around me
> I'm all alone
> In your sanctuary
> No one can see me
> No one can hear me
> Only you hold me
> Only you love me
> Your walls of fabric
> So soft and so beige

Keep me from spazzing

When spreadsheets fill me with rage

[CHORUS:]

Oh Cubie, you see right through me

You promised me privacy

But you handed me lunacy

I will love you until I die

I'll take you with me

Even when they downsize

And then, mid-song, I violently turn on Cubie.

But I know your height

Is a curse so black

Your mediocre walls

Don't keep the vultures back

I came to you, Cubie

For solace and the reasons why

But you can be cruel

And you handed me half a lie!

I'LL TAKE YOU DOWN

I'LL RIP OUT YOUR DRAWERS

YOU'RE DUMB AND YOU'RE STUPID

YOU'RE MADE OF PARTICLE BOARD!

I *knew* it was funny. I couldn't wait to perform it. I had never felt this way. Soon after, I got myself booked on a bringer show, so called because the comedy club gives you stage time in exchange for bringing audience members. Usually it's something like five minutes for five people. If it sounds like a great way to lose friends, it is. This particular show was at the New York Comedy Club. New York. Comedy Club! Not Small Town in the Middle of Nowhere Comedy Club. *New York* Comedy Club. This was top-tier. The big leagues. I invited everyone I knew. I managed to get seventeen people to come.

I showed up that night with my song, "Cubie," on a CD. I was ready to perform along to the track, complete with dance moves. I thought it was odd that New York Comedy Club smelled like dried urine, but there was a painting of Rodney Dangerfield on the wall, so this was for sure *the* place to be. When I got onstage, I was so nervous, my knees buckled. I held on to the microphone for dear life. My dance moves disappeared. I just had to sing this thing and get through it without passing out. And then, something magical happened. I got laughs. Real laughs, and not just from my friends. From strangers! From the other comedians! And I know this is going to sound like I made it up, but when I got offstage, the leathery club booker, Steve, came up to me and shook my hand, and said, "Congratulations kid, welcome to comedy."

I left the club walking ten-feet-tall down Second Avenue, sure that I'd made the right decision to move to this big place with such a big dream. The next day, I made a copy of the VHS tape the club gave me of the performance, and I mailed it home.

"I LOVED IT! Cubie! So funny! AWEsome." Mom gushed on the phone after watching it. "I showed it to my women's Bible study group."

"Oh my god, Mom, that is so embarrassing," I said, unable to contain my smile.

"I explained to them that you *have* to use curse words. It's just part of the business you're in."

Dad got on the phone.

"Way to go, Bo! Particle board! Now *that* is a hoot!"

Soon, Mom visited me in New York for the first time. I showed her my apartment and introduced her to Cubie. That night, she came to see me perform at a show in a theater run by my friend Erik. The tiny space was on the second floor above a seedy locale called Show World. Show World sold adult films and sex toys and still had nickel porn booths. It also used to feature live nude girls in the various performance spaces, but since Giuliani sanitized Times Square in the 90s, the live girls were gone from Show World and replaced by rentable rooms. The only renovation done to our small theater was the removal of stripper poles. The mirrors and disco ball remained, and the black vinyl seating was worn from years of lap dances and furtive jerking off. Inevitably, some men of New York City didn't get the memo about these changes, and almost every time we had a show, at least one would climb the stairs, thinking it was still a strip club.

"No live girls. No nudity," Erik would say immediately, knowing the parched look on a guy's face when he's searching for boobs. "It's a comedy show." The lost man would either slink off in shame, or sometimes defiantly pretend he knew it was a comedy show, buy a ticket, and watch us idiots try out our jokes just so he could save face.

I tried to warn Mom that this would be a creepy location to see me perform solo for the first time.

"I don't care! I think it's funky," she said.

That night, I hosted a variety show for an audience comprised of her and fewer than ten other people. Nobody laughed.

Afterward, I was humiliated and angry that my first big show for my mom went so poorly.

"*I* thought it was hilarious!" she said, "But no one else was laughing, so I didn't know if I should laugh, too! I didn't want to do the wrong thing!"

"It's a comedy show, Mom," I said. "You're supposed to laugh!"

"Shit," I whispered to myself, staring into my desk drawer. There it was, the box of five thousand staples. Empty.

I slammed the drawer shut, hurried to the ladies' room, shut the stall door, sat fully clothed on the toilet, and wept. *You've been working here for* four *years. And have not made* one *dime doing comedy. No prospects. How? How do you make that leap?*

I was performing constantly. By now I was getting booked on numerous stand-up shows in real venues that did not smell like urine and/or the ghosts of sad men. I performed weekly with my improv group and hosted my own biweekly talk show called *Sara Schaefer Is Obsessed With You.* I was even starting to get good press.

"*Sara Schaefer Is Obsessed With You?*" yacht-man boss Gary said, after my face appeared on the cover of *Backstage* magazine. "You should change the title to *Sara Schaefer is* Sexually *Obsessed With You!*"

Gary's awful commentary aside, I felt like I was starting to make real strides. Comedy kept me busy, and Boyfriend was riding high after winning a competition to publish his first novel. It felt like something was going to break big for me, too, if I could just hang on a little longer. Every opportunity felt like purchasing a lottery ticket to an ever-growing jackpot. *If things go just right this time, I win.* Before every audition or job interview, Mom would call or email to wish me luck.

"What are you going to wear?" she would ask. I would promptly describe the new outfit I had bought just for the occasion. After the audition, I'd be on pins and needles for weeks, waiting for the phone to ring, or for an email to appear in my inbox, some word back if I got it or not. I ached for the yes. But then, after a week of radio silence, I'd bitterly ache for a definitive no. I was shocked to discover that standard practice in the industry was to just simply ignore you if you didn't get the gig. Hollywood is not known for precision beheadings. The slower and more painful the spirit-killing, the better.

"I'm gonna come up there!" Mom fumed on the phone after one silent rejection. "I'm gonna talk to them and I'm gonna tell them to stick it where the sun don't shine! Why can't they just let you know you didn't get the part?"

I was sitting in Cubie and didn't have a good answer.

"I don't know!" I said.

One early January evening, my desk phone lit up to reveal my parents' home phone number. I figured it was Mom calling to ask for help with whatever latest project she had taken on, like designing an elaborate flyer for a church potluck or consulting on a catchphrase for the Pennies golf tournament ("Get *teed off* about hunger!").

"Hey, Bo." It was Dad. I could tell something was wrong.

"Hey, Dad. Is everything okay?"

"It's gonna be okay," he said, "but we found out today that Mom has cancer in both breasts."

I tried to un-hear the words.

"No," I moaned.

"Sara." Now, Mom had joined Dad on the line. "Sugah, it's gonna be okay. I'm gonna be fine."

"What did the doctor say?" I wanted details, but really, what I wanted to ask was, *Are you going to die?*

"They have to run more tests and then we will see what the plan is," Dad said.

We sniffled, said our *I love yous*, and threw in another round of *It's All Gonna Be Okays* for good measure. There was nothing to do now but wait.

I hung up the phone and immediately started packing my bag to go home. I stood up and looked around the cubie-hood. The only person still at work was a stiff woman I did not get along with, one of the "vultures" I had referred to in my song. I knew she had heard my phone call.

"I'm going home," I said, holding back sobs. "My mom has cancer."

"Oh, that's . . . awful," she said, like a robot running its empathy sequence.

"Thank you," I replied. We both stared at the wall for a moment, and I left.

The next morning, I made my way back to the office after a sleepless night. I put my iPod on shuffle and closed my eyes, trying not to think about what was going to happen to Mom. As the train barreled into Manhattan, Joni Mitchell's "Both Sides Now" came on, the cruelly beautiful version from 2000, recorded with a complete orchestra behind Joni's aged voice. I looked at my iPod and wondered if some force beyond me had selected the song for me to hear at that very moment. My childhood had two sides —everything before Dad confessed, and everything that happened after—and I feared that at some point in my adult life, a horrible tragedy might open up a new divide, a new line from which to look at both sides now. *Is this it?*

Weeks later, we got word that Mom would need a double mastectomy and a rigorous course of chemotherapy. The cancer was in early stages, but just a little bit had already gotten into her lymph nodes, and, unluckily, she had developed two different types of cancer, one in each breast.

At the hospital before her operation, we stood around her bed in the sterile prep room.

"Do I get a Pound Puppy after this?" Mom joked. In Schaefer-speak, a "Pound Puppy" is any gift you buy for a loved one or yourself in case of illness, career rejection, or personal slight. It originated in the 80s at the Cardinal Drug Store in Sycamore Square, where Mom would take us to pick up prescriptions after doctor visits. This Cardinal was attached to a Ben Franklin store, and combined they sold just about everything. While inside, she'd let us get a Pound Puppy—an adorable line of stuffed puppies with floppy ears and sad eyes that you had to adopt before they got put down.

"Uh, yeah! I think this calls for a really *big* Pound Puppy!" said Dad.

"Shopping spree at Anthro!" I said. In recent years, Mom and I had discovered the retail chain Anthropologie and its offerings of appliquéd bird sweaters and boho chic housewares.

"Yes!" Mom shimmied her shoulders in excitement.

———

Two years passed. The initial plan of attack on Mom's cancer worked, but within a year, the cancer returned and continued to spread. She endured two more rounds of chemo, more surgeries, radiation, and numerous setbacks landing her in the hospital.

Life did not pause for Mom's ordeal. By now, Cristy had two children, and Mom insisted they call her "Lovie," because, to her, "Grandma" sounded old. Jay got promoted at his work and met his future wife, Annie. Ross got a job working with homeless families and met her future husband, Aaron. Boyfriend became Fiancé, and then Husband.

Mom loved every second of it, making sure she didn't miss a thing, even when she wasn't feeling well. Though it was getting harder, she still managed to keep her faith. She described the year after her diagnosis as "the best year of my life," because of the spiritual growth it brought her, and the love she felt from her family, friends, and community. And she never lost her sense of humor.

"I watched the Super Bowl with Daddy this weekend," Mom told me during a particularly rough spell. "The chemo must have given me brain damage because I actually enjoyed it!"

In the whirlwind of it all, I also finally got my big break: that one yes that would change my life. I landed a gig hosting a music-themed online show for AOL. At the time, nobody knew what an "online show" was, including AOL and me, but I was amped to find out. I could finally walk away from Cubie and Gary and nearly five years' worth of staples.

A few months into my AOL job, Mom and Dad visited me in New York. On a break from treatment, Mom was run-down but feeling well enough to travel. She and Dad could not have been more excited for me; in their eyes, I was a celebrity, especially to Mom, because my office was in Rockefeller Plaza, right next to her favorite television program, the *Today* show.

"I got right up to the front!" she exclaimed after going to a taping one morning.

We went on a shopping spree for my hosting wardrobe. We squealed with excitement whenever I found something cute. No matter the shop, Mom would saddle up next to the salesperson and say, "We are looking for things that look good . . . *on camera*," at which I'd feign embarrassment.

"Oh, Sara," Mom would say each time I came out of the dressing room in a new look. Her voice would get low, like she was seeing the sun set over the ocean. "It's . . . gorgeous."

"It fits you perfectly, Bo," Dad would chime in. "And that material is *really* nice. You can tell it's *really* high quality!"

They bought me a few nice things, and I bought myself some, too. The haul was impressive, and I felt like the star Mom had made me out to be.

"I just think you're AWEsome, Sara," Mom said as we sat together on the subway. Dad stood nearby, awkwardly hanging on to a pole with his forearms. He was doing everything he could not to touch any part of it with his hands.

"You set your mind to it," she continued, "and you did it! And your marriage is just *perfect*—"

I winced.

"Don't," I said. A gloom fell over me.

"Well, obviously, nothing is perfect," Mom said, "but you know what I mean!"

"I'm worried it's worse than that," I said.

Over the years, I would sometimes gripe about Husband the way anyone might bitch about the day-to-day annoyances of being in a long-term relationship. But this was different. This was a secret I worried I might not be able to put back in the box now that it was out. I wasn't just complaining about Husband, I was worried that I might have made a mistake marrying him. What I initially thought were normal problems any couple might face (problems that I naively thought would be solved with a wedding) now seemed serious. Each day that went by, it felt like our love eroded a little bit. Instead of growing closer, we were growing apart. My creative life had become increasingly outward facing; there was much more to it now than putting on little shows in a barely renovated strip club. There were so many new places to share myself with the world: social media, TV, blogs, YouTube, the AOL homepage. And now that I had figured out how to make it my actual job, there was no turning back. For the first time in my creative life, I felt truly seen.

Meanwhile, in my home life, I felt unseen. While I pushed myself further into the public sphere, Husband was turning ever inward. He was struggling to sell his second novel and spent more time isolated, writing alone. He did not want to share his work with me, or anyone, and it started to feel as if he didn't want to share anything about his inner life with me. Our secret language still existed, but I needed conversation that went deeper than inside jokes and sarcasm. What once united us was now driving me crazy. I wanted depth. I wanted intimacy. I wanted all of him.

"There's more to marriage than sex, you know," Mom quipped.

"What? Ew! Mom, no!" I hadn't even mentioned sex, even though we weren't having any.

"I know you two love each other so much. And maybe marriage was a mistake. But you are doing the right thing by trying to figure it out. No matter what happens, we love you, and God loves you. He loves you just the way you are."

I could tell she was worried, and I regretted burdening her with it. She had enough to deal with already. Recently, she and Dad had made the painful decision to close The Store and bring an end to Pennies For Heaven. With Mom missing more and more time for treatment and recovery, the entire operation felt rudderless. She wanted to focus on her family, her friends, Jesus, and getting better. We still held on to hope though—after this cancer mess was finally over, she would find some new grand vision to make the world a better place.

When she and Dad left, I could barely stand it. These days, each goodbye felt worse than the last. I visited her often; we talked daily. I did the thirty-nine-mile Avon Walk for Breast Cancer. I put on benefit comedy shows I titled *Cancer Blows*, and I organized a letter-writing campaign for Mom's "basket." The basket was filled with envelopes of letters, inspirational quotes, pictures, cards. Whenever she felt bad, she could reach into the basket and open one. I instructed everyone to put a star on the back of the envelope so she would know it was for the basket when it arrived in the mail. But it still felt like I wasn't doing enough.

It was springtime, and we had planned a bridal shower for Jay's fiancée, Annie, in Richmond. On the day of the shower, Mom was having a bad day, feeling weak and nauseated. After some coaxing, she agreed to go. She could barely get down the stairs, so Jay offered to help. She was frustrated and tried to push him off. He ignored her protests and picked her up, carrying her down the stairs and out to the car.

As I watched him, I felt the weight of her body in my *own* arms. Jay walked silently back up the sidewalk with tears in his eyes.

I knew one day the tables would turn, that I'd experience that moment when the child becomes the parent. But I had always imagined I would have my own head of gray hair when the time came.

At the shower, Mom was loopy. She gave a rambling speech, going around the room telling each person how much they meant to her, except for, inexplicably, Ross.

"What the fuck?" I whispered to Cristy.

"She's out of her mind," Cristy said.

(Years later, Ross told me that Mom had been mad at her, and that's why she had left her out. "I forced her to go that day. She didn't want to and I made her. It was one of the worst days of my life. I did not realize how sick she was." I insisted that none of us did and that it was okay to let it go. "And besides," I said, "remember that time when you were like nine years old, and Mom thought you were faking being sick for like two months, but it turned out you had mono?")

On the way home from the shower, driving down the expressway back to Midlothian, Mom started vomiting bile. We urgently debated if we should take her to the emergency room.

Just then, we heard a hissing noise coming from the back of the car.

"It's the oxygen tank!" I said.

"Um, that's DANGEROUS!" Ross shouted. "Oxygen is explosive! The car might blow up!"

"Oh Jesus Lord, help us!" Mom cried out. "This is the PITS!"

We pulled the car over and called the fire department. As we waited on the side of an off-ramp, I said, "This day sucks."

"Speak for yourself," Ross said. "I'm excited. We are about to see some hot firemen."

Her sense of humor kept us standing as the entire world shook beneath us.

chapter

thirteen

In some parts of the Grand Canyon, the steep cliffs give way to gentler slopes of gravel and dirt, visual evidence of massive landslides. Landslides are triggered by a meeting of water and gravity, or when a tree root squeezes through the rock, cracking it and creating weakness that grows slowly over time. Then, when the structure cannot hold any longer, the cliff gives out, crumbling and sliding thousands of feet downward into the gaping abyss. The landslide dismantles the earth and moves young dirt down to meet the old, creating ferocious rapids, forever changing the landscape.

fourteen

I was completely alone in the waiting room. The test was taking longer than they had told me it would, so I was on edge.

I was not waiting for Mom in this hospital. I was waiting for Dad, who was undergoing some cardiovascular tests. I was alone, because everyone else in my family was at the *other* hospital across town where Mom was still laid up with her infection.

Eventually, a nurse came out and ushered me back to see Dad. When I saw him, he was lying down in a bed with tubes hooked up to him, and he had a look in his eyes I'd never seen before—that of a frightened child.

"Worst-case scenario," he said. "I have to have an emergency triple-bypass. Right away."

The next few days were a blur. Mom tried to rip out her IV to try to get to him. Cristy went into supervisor mode, expertly dividing up duties for us to try and keep Mom calm while also tending to Dad. In one way, the timing of his surgery couldn't have been worse. But in another way, it was divine: his annual checkup had led to more testing, which led to a life-saving intervention. The doctor said he was steps away from a fatal heart attack. Dad had just re-upped his life.

After his surgery I watched him lying there, in a cold and darkened room, surrounded by glowing machines and wires. I watched him sleep, a breathing tube stuck down his throat. I imagined Mom in her room miles away.

None of it felt real.

A few weeks later, Mom was feeling a bit better and was home from the hospital. She asked me to help her with the piles of stuff she kept everywhere in the house—cards she wanted to send, baby pictures of every child born within a ten-mile radius, and an abnormal amount of rooster-themed items. So, we made new, more manageable piles, organized things into proper storage, and threw away a lot of junk.

Then there were the hidden piles. The ones from the past that, in anticipation of company or Dad reaching his limit with her clutter, she'd hastily swept into a suitcase or box and shoved under a bed or into a closet. Every container was a time capsule, a moment of her life preserved. A collection of crumpled to-do lists, unopened mail, church bulletins, photographs, jewelry, entire Bibles, loose dollars and coins, candy, trash, makeup.

Then, we'd open up a closet and see ten more bags of stuff.

"This is SICK!" She'd cackle.

I prefer to remember her cackle that day being loud and full-throated. I choose to see her throwing her hands up in the air and playfully jutting her hip to the side, the way she always did when she felt sassy. But if I'm being honest, her laugh was sleepy, her speech slightly slurred, her body weak. She didn't jut her hip to the side, because she wasn't standing up. She sat in a chair, making executive decisions about each item as I held it up. She couldn't do much lifting, not only from the fatigue but because one of her arms was painfully swollen from lymphedema. After four years of surgeries and treatments—a seemingly endless cycle of victories and setbacks—we were waiting to see if the last round of chemo had done any good. This time, we knew it was a long shot. Just as we uncovered the hidden piles of clutter in every corner of the house, so, too, had the doctors uncovered the disease in every corner of her body.

When we finished cleaning, we lay down on her bed together and talked. The bed was a four-post king-size that was so high off the ground it felt as if you were floating. I pressed my cheek against the blue-and-white patchwork quilt, smooth and cool from the air-conditioning.

I asked her what I was like as a baby.

"You would get so quiet and serious when you were playing by yourself," she said. "At one point, Daddy thought something was wrong with you. I told him, no. She's just focused."

Then, the conversation turned.

"I want Daddy to find someone to love after I'm gone," Mom said. "I want y'all to know that."

"Fine by me. And don't worry, I'll make sure she's uglier than you," I said.

"I'm not afraid of dying. I'm only afraid of pain." This startled me. She'd endured so much pain in her life, physical and emotional. Four natural childbirths. Chronic pain from years of heavy lifting at The Store and manual labor cleaning the church. Tragedies. Loss. Lies. Now, cancer. I had never known anyone who could tolerate so much pain and still manage to be so joyous.

"I just want to make sure that we'll all be together one day, in heaven."

I could tell she needed reassurance that my beliefs aligned with hers. I could have fudged my personal beliefs at that moment, because why fight with your dying mom about the particulars of heaven? But I couldn't imagine lying to her, either. I decided to try to find a way to common ground that wouldn't require dishonesty.

Mom believed in a physical heaven, one that mirrored what it was like on earth, but without all the pain and suffering. Heaven would come fully equipped with an Anthropologie and unlimited Diet Coke. And the way you got there was by believing in Jesus Christ. She knew I didn't attend church, and that I'd stopped wearing my Christian T-shirts and cross necklace during college, but I sensed that she wanted assurances that I believed just enough to get me into heaven.

"I do believe in the teachings of Jesus," I said, my voice tight. "But I just haven't been able to go to a church. I guess I just associate church with bad things. I know you aren't this way, but how on earth is it Christlike to condemn a gay person to hell? I don't get it. Now it's about regulating women's bodies and beating the war drum against Muslims. I liked it better when it was about *love*. That's what Jesus is supposed to be about."

"It's still about that for me. His love is all that matters," she said.

"Well, then, I think, deep down, we believe in the same things. We just use different words to describe them." I pointed to my belief in Jesus's ideas. His radical ideas about love, grace, charity, and peace. I pointed to my belief that living by those ideas releases us from a kind of hell, right now. She agreed with this. Jesus had brought her comfort throughout every hardship in her life.

I told her about a song I'd heard by Ron Sexsmith, in which he says that God takes everyone when they die.

"It's what I have to believe," I said. "I know it might not be exactly what you believe. But it's how I am sure we will be together when it's all over."

"I like that," Mom said. We cuddled for a while, and she fell asleep. I listened to her snoring. It was so soft, like a tiny buzz saw cutting through cotton balls. I wet the quilt with my tears. In that moment I realized how badly I wanted her version of heaven to be real.

A few weeks later, she stopped treatment. A doctor said she could live as long as six months. We were just glad there would be no more barbaric chemotherapy. Maybe she'd have some energetic good days or even weeks. But when the hospice nurse arrived, she observed Mom over the course of a day, and told us she had forty-eight to seventy-two hours left.

I was shocked. Yes, Mom was sick. But not that sick. Yes, she was very weak, but just the other day she was insisting on dressing up and going out on the town. It's the medicine. Yes, she was eating less and less. It's a side effect of a side effect of a side effect. Yes, she was seeing ghosts.

"Did they ever find those children?" she had said recently. "They were just right here, next to me." Spooky as that was, we brushed it off. Mom had always seen ghosts. There was the woman who appeared behind her in her bathroom mirror. Then there was the time she woke up on a balmy summer day and could see her breath in her bedroom, clearly evidence of the presence of some spirit. And who could forget the time she swore she saw a giant alien ship in the sky, forgot about it completely, and didn't remember until there was word of a UFO sighting on the news? Mom seeing things was not out of the ordinary. This was just Mom being Mom.

No matter what the situation, there was always an explanation that wasn't cancer. We thought if we could just resolve this infection here or that complication there, she'd actually be fine. If we could just get her medications sorted, she'd be lucid. So how could this be happening so fast?

The hospice nurse, Sally, had an answer that was cold and simple.

"This is cancer," Sally said. The sentence dropped in my

stomach like a rock in a serene pond. I had been fooled by the disease's slowness. But Sally's cold truth was unexpectedly refreshing after years of dealing with doctors afraid to deliver absolutes. Not only did she provide us with much-needed concrete information but she also cared for my mother in the gentlest way. She talked to and caressed her with the same delicate, warm love you'd give to a newborn baby. I could not imagine a more difficult occupation. And she had to help us, the family members—who could be lousy people!—witness it. *You are an actual angel, and you should be paid millions of dollars for what you do.*

By now, Mom was in a kind of hospital bed in the living room, and it was as if she had been given permission to finally let go. Within a day, she had mostly stopped speaking.

"At any moment," Sally advised, "She could wake up and talk to you. This can happen. Don't leave her alone. Don't assume she's gone."

We never left Mom's side, and at night, we worked in shifts. The dance of my family around her dying body was surreal and sometimes gross and funny and weird and beautiful and terrible.

At 2 a.m., while preparing morphine drops for Mom, we heard a cousin, who was sleeping on an air mattress in the living room, rip a gigantic fart in her sleep. How does one combine the saddest thing you've ever done with the funniest unintentional toot? It was all too much—Cristy, Ross, Jay, and I laughed until we were crying.

The next morning, Sally came in and shifted Mom's body to adjust her bedding. Suddenly, Mom jolted, and she grabbed Sally's arm.

"Not yet! Not yet! Not yet!" Mom cried. Her voice was desperate.

"It's okay," Sally said, as she gently laid her back down. "It's okay now. There, there. You can let go. Shhhhh."

Just as quickly as Mom had startled awake, she slipped right back into peaceful twilight, and those words were the last I would hear her say.

That night, during my 4 a.m. shift by her side, I could tell that she would go soon. I knew the words I said to her might be the last she would hear me say.

"I promise you, Mom," I whispered, just loud enough over the oxygen machine growling in the background. Even with its aid, her breathing was labored and horrific. It was a sound I'd never heard before, but one I knew immediately upon hearing it: it was a death rattle. I grabbed her hand, limp in mine. "I promise, I will stay with him. I will make my marriage work. We will be fine. And we will have babies. I promise. I'm going to be okay. I love you I love you I love you."

I repeated the words like a mantra until my shift was

over. Dad took over for me, and I retreated upstairs. She slipped away at dawn with my dad and aunt by her side, while the rest of us slept.

———

In the week after her death, I felt an odd lightness. I had things to do, people to talk to, gifted barbecue to eat. I had a purpose: I was someone whose mom had just died. But the lightness came from the fact that I was so relieved that she wasn't sick anymore.

There was a strange amount of joy in that time. We cheerfully justified all sorts of self-indulgent behavior by saying, "This is what Mom would have wanted." "Mom would have wanted me to eat a whole pizza." "Mom would have wanted us to get drunk tonight."

Mom would have definitely wanted us to go shopping to buy ourselves some Pound Puppies. If there were ever a time for a Pound Puppy, it was now! So, we hit the mall.

We made a beeline for Anthro. I guess I didn't fully calculate how crazy I would sound sobbing in the middle of an Anthropologie, but thankfully, Anthro is one of those stores where it is quite normal for a woman to break down weeping, even if it's only because she found a wide-legged romper with the absolute *tiniest* deer embroidered on the pocket. I didn't anticipate how shopping there without her for the first time would feel like a sword to my gut. I took a sharp breath and pushed forward. I focused on the clothes, picking dress after dress off the racks. I probably looked like a contestant on *Supermarket Sweep*, stampeding through the store grabbing as many things as possible. I got to the dressing room, arms burning from the load, and found some calm.

But then, there was the flash of a memory.

"I *love* watching your feet under the dressing room stall door," Mom had said once. "They do a little dance as you turn this way and that. I can tell you are trying to see what the outfit will look like from all angles, going up on tiptoes and down again. It just kills me!"

I thought about her sitting outside the dressing room, my feet in that rectangle view, two-stepping with joy like her little girl again. My ankles wobbled under the weight of the memory. I hated not being able to control its sudden appearance and wondered if this was what it would be like, losing her. Going about my life, but then, SURPRISE! A memory comes loose and now I'm leveled.

This is grief, I thought to myself, borrowing Sally's honest tone. After collecting myself, I selected a dress to wear to the memorial service the next day. It was a powder-blue-and-white-striped sundress, its cheerfulness a denial of the darkness left by her absence.

Winfree was packed with friends and volunteers and

some of Mom's Pennies clients that day. One of her clients brought a huge poster-size card signed by hundreds of people she'd helped along the way. The sanctuary was so fat with love, I found it hard to breathe. The legacy of Pennies itself was so strong here. This small thing she did, stopping to talk to men most people would ignore, turned into over a decade of service and over 300,000 meals served. Thousands of shoes and coats donated, even more conversations and hugs. It was incredible to think about all she had done with just a tiny bit of faith. We shook the pew with our weeping.

Family friends read pieces we had written, but Ross somehow mustered the strength to read her own. She talked of a simple memory, on the beach as a child, in Mom's arms, her face against her warm skin, smelling the suntan lotion and the sea.

One of Mom's best friends told a story about Mom putting on a show in their dorm at nursing school. Mom wrote the script, cast the parts, directed it, and produced it. She called it *Pistols & Pettycoats*, inspired by her favorite TV show at the time, *Gunsmoke*. I'd never heard this story before. *So that's where I got that from*, I thought.

We sang Mom's favorite hymn to finish the service: "Just a Closer Walk with Thee."

"When my feeble life is o'er, Time for me will be no

more, Guide me gently, safely o'er, To Thy kingdom's shore, to Thy shore . . ."

Afterward, we gathered in the fellowship hall for food and sympathies. In the days leading up to this, Cristy, Jay, Ross, and I joked a lot about Mom's spirit visiting us. At the funeral home, while a staff member walked us through various cremation options, a fly buzzed around our heads. In such a deafeningly quiet room, this fly was making itself known. It kept landing on different urns.

Cristy muttered under her breath, "Mom? Is that you? Do you want that urn?" We laughed at the idea of Mom's ghost randomly showing up, and how scary that would be in reality. We started making requests aloud to Mom's spirit.

"Mom, please do not be in the bathroom mirror when I come up from brushing my teeth."

"Mom, please don't stand at the end of my bed in the middle of the night!"

"Mom, please don't get inside one of my old dolls and then turn its head real slow-like when I walk in the room."

But on the day of her memorial service, the joke stopped being funny. Too many random women were coming up and saying stuff like "I saw a yellow butterfly on my minivan this morning. It was your Mom!" or "I was washin' my dishes this mornin' and just then a red robin perched upon the windowsill! It was Billie!"

I needed a break, so I retreated to the corner of our church fellowship hall and sat next to my mom's sister, Aunt Anne. Aunt Anne had a mental disability, and she had a beautiful spirit. I knew if I sat next to her, she'd bring me some peace.

"Hi, Aunt Anne," I said.

"Hello," she said cheerfully.

We sat quietly. I stared forward, my eyes puffy from all the crying. I took a long, deep breath and tuned out the chatter in the room. It was peaceful. But then—

"Billie's gone to heaven and she's NEVER comin' back," Aunt Anne declared out of nowhere.

"Billie's gone to heaven and she's NEVER comin' back!" she repeated herself. Her tone was that of a farmer matter-of-factly describing the life cycle of a pig. I almost started laughing, I was so startled by it. She kept going. "Billie's gone to heaven and she's never comin' back. Billie's gone to heaven and she's never comin' back."

An unexpected wave of relief washed over me. *Thank you, Aunt Anne.* It felt like the most honest thing anyone had said to me that day. That's real. That's the truth. Aunt Anne didn't feel the need to resort to fantasy or platitudes.

Billie was gone. And she was never coming back.

That night, I trudged up to my former teen bedroom, which had long been converted into a proper guestroom. I sunk onto the bed and looked wearily around the room. Something on a little wooden cart in the corner caught my eye. It was a Mom Pile. One that we had made on that day of cleaning and talking. It was a to-do pile—pictures she wanted to frame and cards she wanted to send—just sitting there, starting to collect dust. My body seized, throat croaked, rib cage split, my heart forever impaled on a quiet stack of paper. Unassuming and lethal. A humble monument to this church lady in a Wonder Woman belt, a giver and forgiver, a volcano of love, a human cure-all, with so much unfinished business: Lovie. Her legacy here, so plainly piled, whispering the hymn of her miracles unperformed, of her cruelly interrupted adventure. She wasn't done yet. Not even close. Her voice rang out in my head.

Not yet. Not yet. Not yet.

chapter

fifteen

"I want to feel Mom down here," Ross had said at the beginning of the trip.

"Me, too," I had agreed. I had been waiting over ten years
for an official visit from Mom's spirit, but still nothing. I
never got that butterfly moment I was promised by the
church ladies. Sure, I had seen many butterflies over the
years. But none of them gave me strong Mom vibes.

Now, it was the fifth night in the canyon, and I still
hadn't felt anything definitively Mom-like. No bighorn
sheep with her eyes, no clouds in the shape of her head. We

sat in our camping chairs, staring at the black sky, which was crammed with stars. On this stretch of the river, the conditions were just right for a spectacular stargaze. The cliffs sat farther back for a wide scope but were just high enough to keep the moon from barging in too soon.

Andrew was a studious guy and happened to know a lot about space. Someone handed him a (highly illegal) laser pointer, which he could use to point all the way up to the stars as if the sky were a bedroom ceiling.

"Our galaxy is shaped like a flat disk," Andrew explained, "and when you see the Milky Way, it's like you're looking straight *into* the whole horizon of the disk."

This was the first time I had ever felt my physical place in the universe. I could see clear into infinity, and it took my breath away. My eyes went dry as I tried to keep them open, hoping to see some sign of Mom out there. A twinkle here. A shooting star there. Maybe she was waving? I couldn't tell.

Later, on my cot, I used my headlamp to light up my notebook. I tried working on my song for the no-talent show. I knew it needed to be packed with jokes about our journey, while also delivering an emotional punch. I scribbled and scratched lines through words that wouldn't rhyme. I scribbled some more. But nothing felt good enough.

What happens if this song sucks? I asked myself.

Well, then you'll have your answer. Time to give up.

The next morning, during breakfast, Ross approached me at the tent with tears in her eyes.

"Oh no, what's wrong?" I said.

"I asked Tyler to make me an egg," she sniffed, "and he said no." River Daddy was making pancakes this morning, but because of Ross's restricted diet, she couldn't have them.

"But they made you eggs the other day!"

"He must have forgotten. He said that if he made a special order for me, he'd have to do it for the whole group."

"But they *know* you have dietary restrictions, don't they?"

"I mean, I guess!"

Ted had seen the entire thing go down, and approached us.

"Ross, what's wrong?"

"Nothing, I just . . . I can't eat the pancakes. Because of my special diet."

"Oh right!" Ted trotted back to the kitchen and we could see him talking to River Daddy.

"Now they're talking about me!" Ross said, panicking. "I don't want to be drama!"

"Ross, you are *not* drama," I said. "Stating what you need

is *not* drama. You have to communicate with them! Not communicating is what creates the drama! Don't you remember what Ted said at the beginning of the trip? He said that they need *reminding!*"

"I know," she said.

"Look. They spend nine months out of the year sleeping outside on a boat; maybe they have a touch of brain damage? He just forgot!"

"My body is nobody else's business," she said, not appreciating my attempt at humor. "I don't want people looking at me differently."

I wanted to take her hand and drag her up onto a boulder at the edge of camp. I wanted to call everyone over and demand they listen to Ross. I wanted to force her to give a speech about her journey, about her struggle for control over her body. I imagined everyone choking up at her bravery and the group surrounding her in a giant hug. She would feel unburdened, accepted, and truly seen. She would see that no one is judging her. She would be free from shame. She would take control of the narrative. Then I imagined Bob making some inappropriate joke, and then me taking a handful of sand and throwing it into his eyes while River Daddy put him into a headlock. After River Daddy pinned him to the ground, I would put my foot on Bob's neck and say, "If I catch you even *looking* at my sister for the rest of the week, I will come up to your cot while you sleep and cut your throat with the knife she brought."

The scene played out beautifully in my mind. But then I realized a big speech to the group was not her way. It was *my* way—*I* am the one who gets up onstage and shares intimate details of my life.

I thought about when Mom and Dad sent that letter to our friends' parents telling them of Dad's transgressions. How in that moment they tried to control the reaction, to control our narrative. They were just trying to protect us, as I was just trying to protect Ross. But I knew Ross needed to feel in control of her own story and I could not impose on her my ideas of how to fix it.

"You're right," I said. "I'm sorry. It's going to be okay. Everyone here loves you, Ross."

"It's fine," she said, collecting herself. She walked away from me to the water station to fill her bottle. I watched as River Daddy approached her. I could see by his face that he felt terrible. My chest tightened with hope that she would interpret the conversation as a positive and not drama. I could see him apologizing, and her nodding. They hugged, and someone must have said something funny because all of a sudden, they were laughing.

That's my Rossy, I thought.

After breakfast, we packed up and rode the river in the

hot sun. By this point, my skin was a cracked, rashy mess from the endless reapplication of sunblock and a daily battering of sand, water, and wind. My river sandals had given me tan marks that made me look as if I had speckled alien feet. I was starting to yearn for the smaller rapids, because when we hit them, cold river water would rush in the creases of the boat and give my feet momentary relief.

We had recently named our boat Fun Boat, because we were louder and more raucous than the other one. Today was no different, and Fun Boat was alive with chatter, excited for the day ahead. We'd become accustomed to not knowing what was next. We just did what we were told and waited for the next instruction. Everybody hold on; everybody look at these salt crystals forming on the side of the cliff; everybody come look at this four-thousand-year-old pottery shard on which you can clearly see the fingerprints of the woman who made them, the tiny lines of her fingertips repeating the pattern over and over.

"Everybody *look!*" someone gasped.

They were pointing upward toward the cliffs, just before we made our approach to Havasu Creek. I figured it was a bighorn sheep. But instead I saw tents. Another group had set up camp on jagged stone ledges just upriver from Havasu. And there, perched on a cliff just above camp, a beefy man—completely nude—was sitting on a Groover.

"Oh my god, that's incredible," I said. The beefy man did not wave or smile at us, but I could tell that he knew we could see him there, sitting on his throne, taking a shit in front of a group of eighteen strangers riding on the waters below. He had covered his groin with his hands and was very obviously flexing his muscles.

"He's sucking his stomach in!" I howled. "Look at him flexing his pecs!"

"He's kind of hot!" Ross exclaimed. Poor guy—bad timing for Captain Groover; great timing for us.

Soon after, we pulled over to Havasu Creek, a place where aquamarine waters spilled out of a side canyon and collided with the brown of the Colorado, marking the gateway to a kind of secret paradise. We began our hike in, carefully maneuvering narrow ledges and jutting boulders. The waters in Havasu Creek come from deep underground, and the minerals they bring fuse with the air and the rock and give the water its blue-green hue, while also building up travertine, a porous limestone. The travertine terraces created one small cascading waterfall after the next, a true oasis in the red desert.

Finally, we came to a wide set of small falls. At the far-right bank, there was an effervescent emerald pool hugged by rocks.

"Let's do some cliff jumping!" Ted shouted to the group.

He climbed up to a rocky ledge and effortlessly hurled himself off it into the bubbling waters below.

No thank you. Ted had been teasing me for days about how I was, even though I kept telling him that I definitely was not, going to jump off a cliff.

"I'm going," Ross said, with the fixed resolution of a soldier heading onto a battlefield. I watched her climb up the path to the ledge and stand next to Ted, who pointed to the water below. It seemed as if he were giving her a lot of information, which filled me with dread. *Should there be this much instruction?* She looked petrified, but she nodded in determination.

(It reminded me of a story Mom used to tell about Ross when she was little, standing on the edge of a hotel pool in Orlando.

"Hold your breath!" Dad had shouted.

Tiny Ross had looked around and said, "Okay, Daddy. Where is it?")

Ross had that same expectant look on her face as in Florida, but this time there was no Daddy waiting for her below. From my vantage point, the distance from the ledge to the water didn't seem all that dramatic, maybe five feet. But I held my breath nonetheless as she gathered the courage to jump.

"Go Rossy!" I squealed.

Everyone watched and cheered her on. Finally, she squeezed her nostrils shut with her hand and took the leap. The wind flew out of me as I watched her disappear into the frothy jade waters. A split second went by and I imagined her legs shattering against a shallow rock. But then her head popped up and she paddled to the side, beaming and screaming with joy.

"WOOOOOO!" she yelled. I waded over to her to press her for information. I needed to know everything before I would definitely not jump off the cliff.

"It was amazing, Sara," Ross said. "You have to do it."

And then I found myself making the short trek up the rocks to the jumping-off point. A few others were ahead of me, making the leap one by one. My heart beat like a squirrel's. When it was finally my turn, I walked up next to Ted and looked down. It felt a thousand feet high, and the tropical waters below now looked like a violent turbine.

"What the *fuck*, Ted," I said. "How high is this?"

"It's eight feet. Jump *right* there," Ted pointed at a spot. It seemed so specific that if I strayed even an inch, I would crush my spine.

"I really hate that this involves precision jumping," I said.

"You can do this, BoBo," Ted said, unconcerned.

"You got this!" voices behind me muttered, voices I could tell were terrified themselves. Every muscle in my body was buckling, pulling me backward, away from that edge, toward the path back down. Suddenly, I flinched sideways away from Ted.

"DON'T PUSH ME!" I shouted at him, convinced he had changed into a mean frat boy who was about to shove me off for bro points.

"I'm not going to push you!" Ted said. "Trust me, you got this."

I took a deep breath and stepped to the edge.

"GO BOBO!" I heard Ross yell over the falls. "DO IT FOR HANKY!" Hanky, short for Henry, was her son, the youngest nephew in the Schaefer family. I don't know why the thought of an adorable child helps you overcome your fears, but for some reason it did. I held my nose shut and Ted counted down.

"One . . . two . . . three . . . JUMP!"

And I did.

It felt like an eternity between the rock and the water, and when I hit it, I hit it so hard it surprised me. My body shot down like a torpedo, and water blasted up my nose. I scrambled for the open air as if I were dying. Finally, I breached the surface and everyone clapped as I doggy-paddled to the shallow pool. I hadn't felt like this since I was a little kid learning to swim; that desperate thrashing to get to the side of the pool, my head barely above water as

I tried to gain any sense of control. I waded out and looked down at my hands. They were shaking. I never in my life thought I would be able to do something like this, and as Ross took me into her arms, I cried like the little bitch I used to be.

On our way out of Havasu Creek, we passed a number of other groups venturing inward. When we emerged back on the Colorado, Ross tugged at my backpack.

"Sara, did you see who we just passed?"

"No, who?" I figured she had seen a celebrity. *God,* I thought. *I hope it was Christian Bale. I hope he gets separated from his group and we have to bring him onto our boat. And I have to dress his wounds and gently nurture him back to life. It wouldn't be a sexual thing. More spiritual.*

"It was the guy we saw sitting on The Groover!"

"Captain Groover!" I said. "Your crush!"

"No! That's just it," Ross said. "Up close, he wasn't hot at all. I'm so embarrassed! People are gonna be like, 'Oh god, Ross has terrible taste in men.' They're gonna think I have some kind of poop fetish!"

A little later, I stood in the shade eating a ham sandwich. Smoker Bob popped up beside me.

"I was going to ask you," Bob said, his voice made of gravel, "how do you meet guys when you're sober?"

"Oh, I'm not sober," I said, totally unsurprised that he

was interested in my dating life. "I'm just not drinking on this trip. Also, I have a boyfriend, so that part worked out."

"Well, I was going to ask you if you wanted to grab a drink back in Flagstaff after we get back."

"Yeah, I mean sure, maybe," I mumbled. "I'm not sure what my schedule will be, but . . ." I trailed off.

This is the terrible choice women are forced to make when cornered by a sad and clearly lonely man who has no boundaries: Do you outright reject him, and possibly awaken "Mr. Hyde"? Or do you float out a peacekeeping "maybe," and hope that you can pull a vanishing act when the time comes?

"Or maybe we can get more than one drink," Bob went on. "Maybe twenty, so I can get you drunk enough to take advantage!" He let out a bellow and nudged me with his elbow.

"Hahahaha!" Bob laughed, delighted with himself. "You know I'm just joking. You get it!"

Yes, I got it. I laughed along with him, still trying to keep the peace.

"Man, speaking of drinks, I need a Diet Coke," I said. I walked away from him to the raft to grab one out of the soda bag.

Back on the beach, I ran into Andrew and Erin.

"Wait till you hear what Bob said to me this time," I whispered to them, cracking open my can.

By now, all of Fun Boat was keeping record of the creepy comments Bob was making. It had become clear that most of them were aimed at me.

"I'll save it for the boat," I said, looking over my shoulder to make sure he wasn't in earshot.

Back on Fun Boat, with Bob safely on the other raft, everyone looked to me to hear the story. I told it, smiling and laughing as I went. But no one else thought it was funny. River Daddy's face fell.

"Uh, that's not cool," he said. "I have an ax back here. Just so you know."

"This is bullshit, Sara." Ross fumed. "I know you don't like to rock the boat, but I want to say something to him." Now it was *her* turn to step aside and let me handle things my way.

"Look," I said, addressing the group. "I know this type of guy. As a female comedian, you get guys who come to you and think that they can make those types of jokes. They think, hey, she's a comedian, so she can take a joke. I deal with it all the time, and these guys, they're mostly harmless."

"But it's not funny," Matt said.

"No, it's not," I said, starting to feel my face turn red.

Why am I suddenly Bob's PR person? "It sucks, because if you say, 'Hey that isn't funny, screw you, man,' then they go 'Oh, I thought you were a comedian. For someone who pretends to be funny, you are sooo serious.'"

I thought of the hundreds of horrible comments I'd received both in person and online about how I was a shrill humorless bitch for not "enjoying" jokes about my own rape or murder. I felt a little sick—the reaction of everyone in the boat had made me realize how numb I'd become to it all. And how I'd used "humor" to downplay horrible behavior by men all around me.

"I know you feel bad for him," Ross said, "but fuck him forever."

chapter

sixteen

I was in a laundromat in Brooklyn, on New Year's Day, with vomit in my hair, watching my winter coat twist in a dryer, when I told my Dad my marriage was crumbling.

An hour earlier, I'd woken up in my sublet, a cozy room at the top of a Victorian house in Brooklyn. I groaned, suspended briefly in the gap between dark unconsciousness and the harsh reality of life, the moment before the light cut into my eyes, before my head gonged and I smelled something gross. For a second, Mom wasn't dead, and neither was my marriage.

The smell was coming from my hair. Puke. I lay there groaning, trying to piece together the night before. A restaurant. A flash of a friend's apartment. Manhattan. A bar. The futile attempt to get a cab at 12:15 a.m. on New Year's morning. The subway.

The red wine projectile vomit on the orange seats of a Q train.

My sheets, clothes, and winter coat all tainted with barf, I pondered that age-old question: which should I do first: laundry, or shower? I chose laundry. It wasn't my apartment, and someone else lived there. I was in a panic that the stench would seep into the mattress or drift into the common space, so I had to act fast.

While in the laundromat, Dad called.

"Happy New Year, Bo!" His cheer made my head hurt even worse.

"Hi, Dad. Happy New Year," I said, my voice raspy from alcohol and stomach acid. I figured there was no use in hiding my condition. "I'm hungover."

"Well, I'm sure you had fun. You had a lot to celebrate last night! This year is going to be YOUR year!"

Twenty-four hours earlier, I had received the news that I had landed a gig as the head blogger at the forthcoming *Late Night with Jimmy Fallon*, a dream job and huge step up for my career.

My work life had been a roller coaster since Mom died; two weeks after the funeral, AOL had canceled my show, and I had to briefly go back to being a financial researcher. Thankfully, a blogging gig for the VH1 comedy show *Best Week Ever* saved me from getting stuck there for too long, and within a year of that job, I got *Late Night*. But as my career leapt upward, my marriage kept sliding downhill, and by early November, I had moved out to get some space and try to figure things out.

"Well," Dad shifted into his serious voice. "I also hope that maybe this new year will bring healing to your marriage."

I blurted out the truth.

"Dad, I know this isn't easy to hear. But I think it might be over. I think we might get a divorce."

It was hard to even utter that word, divorce. Divorce was totally against the rules, the very definition of Bad. No one in either of our immediate families had ever gotten divorced. For years, I wouldn't even let the word enter my mind, and instead would fight like hell to bridge the gap between myself and Husband. I would beg and cry and scream, but it often felt as if I were shooting arrows at a massive concrete wall.

I tried changing myself. Perhaps the old adage "you can't change a man" was true, so why not start with me, the woman? I thought that maybe if I could make it big in my career, we would have more money, more freedom, and that would change things. So, I threw myself into it even harder.

I tried radical acceptance. *I guess we are asexual. We are not a couple who physically touches each other. That's just who we are. We don't do that. Fuck the haters, not each other! We're* fine.

We were definitely not fine.

Finally, I let that word come to the front of the line: divorce. *But we made a vow! Doesn't that mean something? Could the vows themselves be the bridge across this great divide?* At our wedding, we had sworn to everyone that we would stay together until death did us part. The only way this relationship was going to end was if somebody died. It sounds grim, but that's the deal. *It doesn't matter if you're miserable.* I thought about what I had said to Mom in the last hours of her life. *You made a promise. All that matters is that you keep it.*

I did everything you were supposed to do. Be a good girl. Meet "the one." Fall in love. Get married. So why did I feel so incredibly alone? I thought about running away. *What if I pretend I'm dead, and just start over in a new town under a new name? Surely that would be easier than a divorce.* I had never broken up with anyone before, so not only did I have no idea as to how one goes about doing it, but I also had no clue as to how you can tell when it's over. I did not trust my feelings.

At night, I would lay awake listening to him sleep beside me. Inside, the debate would begin:

I can't breathe. (Really? How weak are you? Try breathing harder.)

I'm unhappy. (You have zero right to be unhappy. Look around at everything you have.)

I have to get out. (The Crock-Pot. What about the Crock-Pot? Somebody gave us that Crock-Pot from your greedy wedding registry. They gave it to you under the condition that you'd stay together forever. You won't only be breaking the promise you made to him, you'll be breaking the promise you made to Mom, your family, his family . . . and the person who gave you the Crock-Pot.)

Then, I simply broke. I did something so far outside my personality, so far off my narrow moral path, so against my strict code of conduct, it was as if I were possessed.

I slept with someone who was not my husband.

I did not plan it. There was no drawn-out courtship, no grappling with "should I or shouldn't I," no falling in love. Instead, something unhooked inside of me one night after a comedy show. I went up to a guy—who I could tell liked me—and asked him if he wanted to grab a drink. When the question came out, it was as if someone else were speaking. I waited for the rush of regret, the chance to change my mind before it was too late, but it never came. I unzipped the skin I'd been wearing for thirty years, stepped out of it, and walked blankly and robotically into the arms of another man.

For the first time in my entire life, I wasn't thinking of anything at all. I was physically and mentally naked with this other person, who was, to be clear, practically a stranger. My brain, *for once*, was empty from the nonstop negative voices, devoid of judgment and intention. Tonight, I was my body, not my thoughts. I was shocked at how easy it was to just step over one of the biggest rules there is.

Just like that, *thou shall commit adultery*.

When I woke up the next morning, I hit the ground hard. The thoughts violently returned, like a high-speed train you don't see coming. *What have you done? What have you done? What have you done? You are a cheater. An adulterer. Some places still execute women for doing this. Some men murder women for doing this. Go ahead. I deserve it.* I had just thrown a lit match onto a gasoline-soaked pile of bone-dry wood. There was no going back now.

In the days after my betrayal, I could barely eat, and my eyes were black. Shame engulfed me. But down at the bottom of my gut, something else was happening. There was a spark of something new: the idea that I deserved to be happy. And that maybe, the only way to be happy was to leave him. It felt like an enormous gamble. I thought of the things people always say: "The grass is always greener." *I just took a little walk on that grass, and I won't lie, it is quite green!* "Marriage isn't easy. You have to work at it." *I have given everything I have to this relationship. What else is there to give? The canyon is here now between us.*

I told him I needed a trial separation. I had never lived alone, and I yearned for that freedom. I wanted to find out who I really was, without him next to me.

"You know, Mom and I survived tough times," Dad said, as I stared at the clothes tumbling in the dryers. I could hear the disappointment in his voice, and I felt as if I were going to throw up again. "She forgave me. And she loved me unconditionally."

A flash of anger tore through me. I couldn't tell him that I felt like I was the one who needed forgiving. I had yet to tell anyone what I had done, much less admit it to my father. I couldn't tell him all of the thousand things that added up to that night with the Man Who Was Not My Husband and now this moment here in the laundromat.

A memory appeared: my parents kissing each other in the kitchen of our house in Salisbury. I longed for that kind of intimacy. My parents fought sometimes, but never stopped communicating and sharing who they were with each other. I never once questioned if my parents loved each other. I wanted my love to be that obvious. I wanted to scream at my father that not every marriage is the same. Love is universal, but relationships are peculiar.

"Maybe," I huffed. "Maybe I'm leaving him *because* of you and Mom. Maybe I want that kind of love." Even though I wasn't sure I deserved it.

I resented him for holding Mom over my head in that moment, but he wasn't the first person to do it. Several people had suggested that this divorce was simply a child of my grief. And it was true that Mom had died at age sixty-two—I couldn't help but start thinking this was also my own life expectancy. At thirty, it was unsettling to think that I was already halfway done. Life suddenly felt very short, and I wanted to make sure I didn't waste another second convincing myself that being *this* unhappy was somehow normal. Mom dying wasn't the cause, but it may have been the catalyst to make a change.

Every time I explained to someone why we were breaking up, I was faced with disbelief. Partly because it contradicted the "perfect love" I had worked very hard to project to the world, but also because, as it turns out, people still hold very traditional beliefs about what is a "good reason" for divorce. Feeling so suffocatingly lonely and depressed that I regularly fantasized about faking my own death is, apparently, not a good enough reason.

"Your mom died, that's why." (No.)

"Is he gay? He must be gay." (Also no.)

"You recently went off birth control—perhaps that's making you unstable?" (Okay, now, hang on. I asked my gynecologist if this could be true. She chuckled as she assured me that no, this was most likely not the reason I was leaving my husband.)

I wondered if these interrogations were something women deal with more than men. As women, we can't possibly just *know* what's best for our own lives. And when we put ourselves *first*? Look out! A feral—potentially evil—woman is on the loose! Still, these questions slithered into my psyche and cozied up to my shame.

I tried to hide what I had done from Husband for a time. I convinced myself that it would only hurt him more. I lied to myself that it was purely for his own protection, when in reality, it was also for my own. I could not believe that I, a Good Girl, had done something so unequivocally Bad.

I did not know that he was conducting his own investigation. He accessed my email, social media accounts, and phone records, and figured out what I had done. When he confronted me, he almost seemed euphoric. I don't blame him. I could easily imagine it being a sort of relief, uncovering the confirmation of a suspicion and that rush of Being Right. He had found the reason! But instead of pushing me away, he offered instant, blanket forgiveness. Now I could return to him, he said. Now we could heal, he promised, like a wise king bestowing mercy on a beggar thief. I sobbed as I apologized over and over again. And I trembled as I told him that I could not give him what he wanted; I was not sure I could come back to him.

From that point on, everything exploded. What was once a mature dialogue about how we had both contributed to the problem was now a manic hunt for the source of my bad behavior. But there was no satisfactory end to this search. My terrible choice destroyed any chance of an amicable split and overshadowed every step forward. Now, I had to accept that there was only one official cause for our split: me. The villain.

"Okay," Dad said, realizing I was not going to magically heal my marriage after one short conversation with him about Mom. After a long pause, he said, "Well I love you no matter what you decide to do."

"Thank you, Dad. I love you, too."

We hung up. I fought off more waves of nausea as the reality of my life sunk in. Telling my father that I was probably going to get a divorce made it feel real for the first time. And not being able to tell my mother was excruciating. I wanted to explain it to her, all of it, and wished I had while she was still alive. Maybe if I had, I wouldn't have made those stupid deathbed promises. Maybe she would have helped me do this the right way. I wanted her to deal with Dad for me. She was the one who would take the unpleasant stories of my life and explain them to Dad. He and I butted heads about everything from burnt lasagna to politics, and she had softened our edges. But now I had to face him directly, and I couldn't bring myself to tell him the whole truth.

More than anything, I wanted her to tell me it was going to be okay. I was going to have to find a way forward without her help. When my laundry finished, I bought myself a Diet Coke and went back to my apartment to take a long, hot shower and scrub the smell of puke out of my hair.

chapter

seventeen

The Groover was now so full of foul odors that I would gag every time I used it. Even if I breathed through my mouth, the toxic gas radiating out of that thing could asphyxiate a whole city.

This was the seventh and last full day of our trip. Ross and I completed our morning routine with expert speed: after breakfast, I held a towel up around her while she put her contacts in, shielding her eyes and fingers from grains of sand flying in the morning breeze. I quickly dismantled the tent, rolled it up, and pressed the air out of it with each turn, and she held the bag while I slid the dense cylinder of fabric inside. We dropped our belongings into our dry bags, folding the wide openings down and clicking their buckles tight. Then I had one more daily ritual to perform: checking to see if Spandad was still wearing the same outfit. He was.

Today we would be running the most famous rapid on the river: Lava Falls. A Class X, it was as if God had planted this rapid here for the ultimate climax to our adventure. As we got closer, I noticed the landscape changing, now dominated by shiny black rock. Matt stood on the back of the boat and described what we were seeing. The day before, one of the women on the trip had put his long, yellow hair into two braids, making him look more like a Viking poet than I thought possible.

"Basalt is hardened lava," Matt said. "Many times, the ancient volcanoes erupted, and the lava would flow down into the canyon and create gigantic dams, which would hold back the water, forming huge lakes. Eventually, the dams would break and send millions and millions of tons of water flooding the canyon below."

The basalt sparkled in the morning sun. Soon, we lost sight of Ted's boat as the river curved ahead of us, and something in the atmosphere shifted. Just as we began to hear the sound of waterfalls, a huge black rock appeared in the middle of the river.

"This is Vulcan's Anvil," River Daddy announced. The volcanic remnant loomed before us, rising fifty feet out of the river, as if to warn us of the dangerous waters ahead. As we quietly floated around the rock, gazing up at it, the sound of the turbine below grew louder. I could feel my ears tighten as the air pressure changed, and I gulped down that now-familiar feeling of inevitability, the accelerating current of the river taking us hostage once again. I assumed my two-hand-hold position long before it was necessary.

"Lava Falls is big and fast," River Daddy said. "Get ready for a fun ride!"

I looked around the boat. Everyone leaned forward, gripping various ropes and straps. Some were making last-minute adjustments, lodging their arms underneath a strap while trying to hold up a GoPro as others tightened their hat strings. I leaned into Ross's body, which had become my shield on almost every rapid thus far. I watched Erin, who had opted for the brave front seat, twist her wrist beneath a strap for extra security. Everyone looked determined but unafraid. We were ready to make our passage.

We fell silent as the thrashing waters roared before us.

"HANG ON EVERYBODY!" River Daddy yelled as we descended into Lava Falls. The waves clapped against us, and then the raft tipped straight upward into an angle I knew meant for a huge drop on the other side. We flew downward, into a mountain wave that crested over and then engulfed us completely. Soon, we fell into another massive hole, this time even bigger than the last. When we emerged back out into the open air, I saw Erin's arm still grabbing the rope, but her seat was empty. The crash of the wave had thrown her down between the front lip and side pontoon of the raft.

"Erin!" Ross shouted. Andrew pulled her back up just before the next wave hit, which was fortuitous, because she was in danger of being sucked under the boat. Erin smiled as she repositioned herself back into her seat, so I knew she was okay. Everything was happening so fast, and I was so busy focused on the fact that Erin had almost been tossed overboard that I hadn't noticed that the boat was going in the wrong direction. Instead of pointing downriver, we were spinning in the churn and now barreling straight toward the left bank. I listened for the sound of the engine revving, but it was eerily absent. River Daddy had no control over the boat.

"Hold on!" River Daddy barked. "There's gonna be a bump!"

With no ability to slow down or change course, we crashed head-on into a narrow embankment covered in shrubs. The force of the bump surprised me; we were going much faster than I realized, and our bodies flung sideways. River Daddy wrestled with the sputtering engine, but it was immediately clear that we were stuck. *Oh my god*, I thought. *Are we going to have to spend the night here on the boat?*

Matt scrambled to the front of the boat with a rope. Everyone sat in total silence, suddenly aware that we might be in danger. Almost instantly, Ted's boat vroomed up beside us. All four guides flew into action with barely a word; clearly, they had trained for moments like this. They attacked the problem with ropes and hooks, their bodies clashing with the sharp branches on the craggy shoreline.

THWACK! Suddenly, a rope sprung lose and struck me across my arms and legs like a bullwhip. It burned like a hot poker and I looked down as I watched the puffy red outline of a rope bubble up on my skin. Despite the pain, part of me hoped it would permanently scar. I started writing the tall tale in my head as we sat there. *"Oh, this scar?"* I would say as children of all ages gathered at my feet in front of the giant fireplace in my supersized log cabin. *"I forget that it's even there."* My gaze would trail out into the horizon, as I'd gently push up my winter shorts, revealing the full extent of the branding. *"This is the price I paid for saving the lives of myself and twelve others deep inside the Grand Canyon. Had it not been for my outstretched leg, the rope would've snapped clean through the raft, leaving us to drown in the muddy water below."*

Eventually, the guides dislodged our boat and River Daddy revived the engine—the crisis was averted. The red marks on my skin were already fading. There would be no scars as visual aids in my future storytelling.

Just after Lava Falls, there is a calm-looking stretch of water, just before Lower Lava Rapid, a Class V.

"Looks like Ted's gonna bump into the cliff!" said Matt.

I looked downriver and could see Ted's raft drifting toward a sheer stone wall. He had tried to idle there, waiting to make sure we came along without any further trouble, but the flow of water was pushing them sideways.

The boat hit the wall, bounced outward, and Dan, sitting at the very front of the boat, lost his hold and ricocheted off the raft and into the water.

We gasped in horror, and I watched Shelly try and fail to catch his hand as he slipped below the surface. Her screams of terror echoed off the rocks. We were too far away to do anything to help, so we sat in powerless silence as Dan disappeared into the muddy river.

Suddenly I realized how violent the "calm" river here actually was. I remembered one of the guides describing this phenomenon: After a big rapid, a flat patch of river indicates a powerful upwelling of water that spreads along the surface. Though it looks peaceful, it is anything but, and at its edges, the upwelling needs somewhere to go: back down.

"Please come up, please come up," someone said urgently.

Dan was not coming up. It occurred to me that I might

be watching someone die, and in an instant, all of the fun of the entire trip evaporated. Time slowed down; each second that passed felt longer and longer. Ten seconds went by, and still no Dan. Ten seconds doesn't sound like a long time, until it is the amount of time someone you know is under the water of one of the world's most powerful rivers.

After that decade-long ten seconds, Dan's tiny head finally emerged.

"Oh, thank God!" I said. He splashed his arms and then, as suddenly as he had resurfaced, the current pulled Dan down underneath again. Lower Lava Rapid roiled up ahead.

By now, Ted had quickly maneuvered the boat downriver, turning it to face where they anticipated Dan would come up again, if he came up at all. Jesse was perched on the edge, ready to grab him.

After another eternity, Dan popped up a second time and raised an arm into the air. Jesse grabbed hold and, with one tremendous tug, yanked him onto the boat like a huge floppy tuna pulled from the sea.

We all exhaled in spontaneous relief.

"Thank you, Jesus!" I shouted to the sky. As we continued downriver, I trembled, thinking of how close we had just come to tragedy. All of my fears of the first day came rushing back, in even more vivid intensity.

Both rafts came ashore in a small inlet. Here, we would

stop for lunch, and presumably try to process what we had just witnessed. But first, Ted made an announcement.

"Things got a little spicy back there, didn't they?" he said with a slight smile. I wondered if people often fell overboard, or if he was just pretending that this was fine.

"Well," Ted continued, "all the more reason to take a moment and congratulate y'all for surviving Lava Falls. As is tradition, you are now officially River Rats. Welcome to the club!"

With that, he handed a small baggy over to River Daddy. River Daddy took the bag and passed it down to us. Inside was a pin for each of us, golden and in the shape of a tiny rat.

"This pin means you're part of an exclusive club," River Daddy said. "Now, when you're back in the real world, and you see someone else wearing the pin, you know you've both done this rare thing. Always wear the pin with the rat's head pointing up, for good luck to all the other River Rats that might be down here. If he's facing down, he might drown."

I rubbed my finger over the tiny golden rat and thought of Dan's head popping up above the water. *Head up*, I said to myself, firmly.

As soon as we got off the boats, we circled around Dan to hear him describe the ordeal.

"I hate to admit this," Dan said, as Shelly stood next to him. She was clearly shaken, but her hair and makeup still looked flawless. ". . . but I broke the one rule. I wasn't holding on. And let me tell ya, it was like being in a washing machine down there. I had no control. The second time I got pulled under, I thought, I can only do this once or twice more, and then I'm a goner. This is why you want your life jacket to be very tight."

Shelly turned away and started crying. I worried for her mascara.

"Jesse," Dan said, "thank you for saving my life, man."

Lunch was now ready, and we lined up to wash our hands and build our tuna salad sandwiches. As I waited for my turn, Dan's words echoed in my head. *No control.* Had we survived Lava Falls, or any of this, because we were special? Brave? Skilled? Or had we survived because we were lucky? Because the Grand Canyon decided to *let* us live? I flashed back to the engine giving out. To Erin slipping off her seat. To me jumping into a rock-filled pool. To Ross following a black light around at night looking for deadly insects. I looked at the ancient lava all around us and wondered when those volcanoes might wake up again. I thought about all the lies we tell ourselves to feel safe.

Who did we think we were?

eighteen

Who do you think you are?

It was a thought I had frequently after the divorce. Every day was a confluence of emotions, from poison shame to confetti joy. I needed a way to navigate them.

I started by erecting an ethical wall inside myself: aside from conversations with friends and family, I was to never publicly speak about Husband or our marriage. But all the gnarly details of everything that happened after? That was easy. In the years after the divorce, onstage and on podcasts, I shared the most intimate details of my new sex life. (And for that, I would like to apologize to my family, who had to listen to me describing squirting as "a water balloon popping between my legs" on my first comedy album.) It was an explosion of creative freedom and inspiration, and audiences were lapping it up. (I am so, so sorry.)

On the other side of the wall was a past cloaked in darkness. Even though sometimes I would try to talk about it in the vaguest of terms on podcasts, I still felt uncomfortable saying anything beyond "I was married, and now I am not," and I would carefully censor myself in any public conversation about the topic. The wall went up in part, because during our separation, Husband had demanded, in his anguish, that I promise to never speak about him publicly or in any of my future work, even asking me to sign a legal document attesting to such. I refused to sign it, but I tried to assure him he had nothing to worry about. From then on I was terrified of breaking those assurances. I am still terrified.

The wall also went up because of an incident that happened one day during our separation, soon after he confronted me about my infidelity. I was on a party bus filled with *Late Night* writers, producers, and Jimmy Fallon himself. Jimmy had taken all of us on a retreat to Atlantic City for the weekend, a chance to bond before the premiere of the show. The entire weekend felt like a validation of my dreams, and I was buzzing with excitement to be a part of it.

We were on our way back to New York, and just as we were pulling into a rest stop on the New Jersey Turnpike, I got a text from Cristy:

Please call me. No one is hurt, but I need to talk to you as soon as possible.

I figured someone had been in a car accident, or fired from their job, or worse. Was someone going to jail?

When the bus door opened, I rushed out and called Cristy.

"First of all," she said urgently, "I want you to know that it is going to be *okay*. Jay, Ross, and I debated telling you, but we think you need to know." Husband had contacted all of them and told them I had cheated on him.

"He is threatening to tell Dad next," she said.

It had not even occurred to me that the bad news might be about me. At first, I could not speak. Eighteen-wheelers and cars whizzed by on the highway. The tremor started in my feet and rumbled all the way up to my head. It felt like the asphalt might crack open underneath me and swallow me. I couldn't find my breath in the February air.

"Why?" I finally croaked. "This is between me and him. Why would he do this? I was going to tell you, I just—"

"I know, I know you would have," Cristy said, without a

hint of judgment in her voice. "I think he thought maybe we would take his side and intervene on his behalf? He said you were suicidal and on drugs, which I know you are not."

"WHAT? I am definitely not suicidal or on drugs! Where did he get that idea?" *Ah, there it is: the good reason for my bad behavior. I'm mentally ill, and on drugs.*

"I don't know. Sara, I think I said, 'How DARE you?' fifty times. I told him nothing you could do would matter to us. I told him to NEVER call me again."

Cristy's voice felt so far away. I watched as the last of my coworkers, Michael, reboarded the bus. He turned and saw me and waved me over. I could not open my mouth to scream right now. I could not stay on the phone and let Cristy's soothing words wash over me. I could not do anything but tighten every muscle in my body to keep it from collapsing.

"I have to get off the phone," I said. "I have to get back on a bus with Jimmy fucking Fallon! What the fuck!"

"I'm so sorry Sara," Cristy assured me. "Call me when you get home."

I hung up, boarded the bus, and took a seat near the front. Everyone was tired and hungover from the weekend, so maybe if anyone saw my pale face, they would assume I was holding back vomit for the same reason they were. I turned to look out the window. The ugly landscape of chemical plants of Elizabeth, New Jersey, and the trash caught on brown winter branches, matched how ugly and dead I felt inside.

I imagined him telling my dad. Was he doing it right now? I felt exposed and condemned. *How stupid, to think you could hide this.* How embarrassing, like a poorly forged signature on a Talky Turtle. That line from Mark's Gospel rang in my head: *Whatever is hidden away will be brought out into the open, and whatever is covered up will be uncovered.*

Bzzzz. My phone vibrated. It was a text from Jay.

I want you to know that I love you and I have your back.

Bzzz. Another text, this time from Ross.

I don't care what you did. I will destroy him.

Bzzzz. Cristy.

It's going to be okay, I promise.

Each text was a life-saving injection, but I was crashing too hard to feel them yet. I twisted my body even farther away from the group so that I could cry. *Perfect timing*, I thought. *What better place to have a complete nervous break-*

down? On a party bus with your brand-new coworkers at your dream job, who happen to be elite comedy writers, cool stand-up comics, and one celebrity. Out of the corner of my eye I could see Jimmy dancing. I clutched my phone, drinking in these texts from my siblings, the antidote to a poison of my own making.

That night, I took the Q train home to my new sublet in Brooklyn. This one was closer to Manhattan, which meant that in order for me to afford it, it had to be slightly shoddier than the last. My room had only a bare mattress on the floor. It felt like the appropriate bed for a Cheaty Cheetah like me. How far this Talky Turtle had fallen.

In the days after, I found the courage to tell Dad everything. Whatever Cristy had said to Husband was sufficient enough to hold him off, and I was grateful for the chance to at least control the way my father found out about my illicit sex life.

"We all make mistakes," Dad said, uncomfortably. I don't think he expected this from me, and there is no way to tell your Dad that you cheated on your husband without it being the most awkward conversation of your life. But he also did not sound disappointed, the way he had many times over the years when I had made far lesser mistakes. To my relief, he did not employ his Dadisms. No "It's all about choices" or "With opportunity comes responsibility." Instead, he simply said, "All you can do is just move forward, try to learn from it, and find a way to forgive yourself."

This time, Dad was speaking to me as an equal, a comrade in the morality wars. Now, he was not my father or judge or keeper. He was simply telling me what had worked for him. I had always imagined his path to redemption to be straightforward: pay the money back, no matter how long it takes, one check at a time, and then it will be over. It took him a long time, and it wasn't easy, but he did it. But now I realized that there was this other debt he had to pay, the one he owed himself.

I had no dollar amount to work toward, no metric for making things right with Husband—soon to be Ex-Husband. But even if I did, I would still have to figure out how to forgive myself. I had no idea how to even begin.

For now, I allowed myself to feel the warm acceptance of my family. They each held me in their grace and supported me as I walked forward into my new life. I did not feel deserving of their love, but they were giving it to me anyway. *This* was that unconditional love Dad was talking about that day in the laundromat. *This* was family, this was Mom, this was Jesus.

After Husband exposed me, I knew exactly what it felt like to have your dirty laundry aired all over town. I knew the loss of control, and the fear that stays with you for

months, even years after. The fear of *What will he do next?*
The fear that you are being watched. The fear that you have
no privacy, no safe place to make mistakes. And the idea
that you deserved all of it, and that the rage you sometimes
feel toward him is not allowed. You imagine the pain you
caused him, and hear a voice, ever-present, whispering in
your ear: *This is what you get.* I felt if I revealed anything
about him publicly, that I would be betraying him again, or
worse, attempting some childish retaliation. Even if it was
my truth, it was a truth that could not be told without hurt-
ing him again. And I, the villain, had no right.

So I folded up everything about him into a box and
shoved it into the back of my mind. I told myself that the
box was just there to ensure that I didn't accidentally spill
the goods. *You have always been an oversharer, so we will need
to take precautions.* What I didn't realize was that it was also
a convenient way to avoid thinking about it at all. It allowed me to turn my attention to the bullet-train pace of
my brand-new life. I jam-packed my days with work and
my nights with performing, hanging out, and hooking up.
Every day was filled with exciting new experiences, a whirlwind of learning that tricked me into thinking I was really
getting somewhere.

"You're growing up," my therapist would say, no matter
what story I had just told her. It was all she ever really said to

me, and I found myself canceling our sessions more and more. It was hard to prioritize taking my lunch break to go see her each week, when so many cool things were happening at my job. When the show's producer asks you if you want to run downstairs and interview Tina Fey for the blog, you cancel therapy. When Jimmy calls you into his office to see if you'd be willing to play a witch on tonight's show, you cancel therapy. When there are free Cronuts in the conference room, you cancel therapy.

My achievements in my career only confirmed my decision to shove everything into that box. I was winning Emmy Awards. After two and a half years working at *Late Night*, I landed my first official TV writing job at *Who Wants to Be a Millionaire*. I met a handsome and kind man named Scott, and our love was both easy and deep. He was a comedian and producer, like me, with aspirations like mine. I started a podcast with my friend Nikki Glaser, and people really liked it. I booked my first stand-up tour.

And then Nikki and I sold a pilot for our very own talk show to MTV. It all felt like proof that I had made the right choices. *You're growing up*, I told myself.

Whenever I felt sad, or a little nag that maybe I wasn't quite right, instead of going to therapy, I went shopping. Pound Puppies seemed like a more convenient fix for any feelings of despair, even if it meant losing total control of my finances. I never stopped to figure out how much it would actually cost to live alone, especially on the modest salary these new TV jobs afforded me. Pretty soon, I was putting groceries on my credit card, and what was once just a large pile of student loans now included close to $40,000 in credit card debt. Every month I felt as if I were carrying a cup filled to the brim with liquid that would spill over at even the slightest jolt to my life, and every month, I wondered if I'd able to cover it all. I took on all kinds of side gigs to make ends meet. I videotaped a monthly erotic reading series my friend ran at a bar called Happy Ending, which, if the name didn't already tip you off, is one of the skeeviest bars in all of Manhattan. I wrote rhyming poems for rich people, which is actually a job. I wrote funny speeches for wealthy men who wanted to impress other wealthy men. I sold my barely worn Anthropologie clothes to girls in Iowa on eBay.

With my debts at their limits, and my calendar stuffed full, I did not have the time or space to calculate the damages of a death and a divorce. I started running a few days a week, though I am unsure if what I was doing could be classified as actual running. It was more like a shuffle. As I shuffled around my neighborhood, I would listen to an Ellie Goulding song on loop. She would sing, "Without your love, I'm getting somewhere!" It became my mantra. *Without his love,*

I'm getting somewhere. It's funny, because the next line in the song is "Without your love, I'm feeling so bad." But for some reason I couldn't hear it.

There were other things I couldn't hear. For example, this is a stand-up joke I used to tell, and it is based on a true story.

When I turned thirty, my Number was one. Not my Sleep Number, but the number of people I'd had sex with up until that point . . . was one. And I was looking to greatly increase that number in a very short amount of time. I had seen all of Sex and the City, *plus the movies. I was ready. I felt like I had a lot of catching up to do. A lot of things to check off my Fuck-It list.*

One of the things I thought everyone had done was have a one-night stand with a total stranger that they had just met. I thought that was just something everyone had already done. So I was like, "Oh I gotta go get that taken care of," like it was a cavity I had to go get filled. Literally.

So I go to a bar, and I find a guy who I think is pretty cute. I'm not gonna lie, I was hitting on him pretty hard. And by that I mean, I just stood next to him until the end of the night. And we went to his hotel—what could go wrong?—and I don't mean to get too graphic here, but we were full-on doin' it. And it was great. *Not only because of the stranger danger, but also because we were very well matched, age-wise. He was twenty-three, and I was thirty, both at our respective sexual peaks. I didn't feel so much like a cougar as I did a she-wolf. Seriously, if you're single, you have got to get yourself some of that tight, young penis. That shit is goooood. It was everything I imagined the one-night stand to be.*

At this point, I thought to myself, hey, we're here, and we're sex gods, so why not take this to the next level? *I decided to put in a request. I put on my sultriest voice possible. Remember what Kathleen Turner sounds like? Okay, now go ten octaves lower.*

I said, "Why don't you be a little rough?"

Now, in my mind, "a little rough" meant one of the following:

+ *Light tugging of one section of your partner's hair*

+ *Correcting your partner's posture by gently pushing their shoulders down*

+ *Whispering to your partner that they are "so bad"*

+ *Putting your hand around your partner's throat with the same pressure you might give a raw egg or bouquet of baby's breath*

Well, he didn't do any of those things. Instead, he immediately, without saying anything, punched me in the face. *There was no hesitation, no discussion, no clarification. He heard the word "rough" and instantly clocked me in the jaw with the business end of his palm. I'd never been truly hit in the face before. And let me tell ya! It is just like the cartoons! I was all like "BYONG YONG YONG YONG! [cuckoo-clock sound effect] [little birdies flying around my head]."*

That's when I learned you should always have a safe word. Mine is "don't punch me." Which I realize is more than one word, so that's why I made it into a portmanteau: "dontpunchme."

Now, this is going to sound controversial. But hear me out. In a way, I did kiiiind of ask for it. I know. You're never supposed to say that after a woman gets hit! But if you really think about it, it's true! I asked for it, in the same way, let's say, if you went to a fancy restaurant, and you said to the waiter, "Have the chef surprise me." And then, the waiter brings you a plate of steaming human feces. In a way, you did ask for that. You are surprised! He was rough. Now, some people get worried about me when they hear that joke. But I just tell them, don't you worry about me. He's dead.

It has all the makings of a great stand-up story: my late-bloomer naïveté about advanced sex moves, an awkward mishap amid the sloppy collision of junx, and that ever-impactful surprise punch line, literally.

But whenever I got up onstage and gleefully told this story, I did not stop to think about what it really meant. It wasn't until years later, when I was on Twitter, reading yet another woman's story of sexual assault, that it occurred to me, for the very first time, that I may have been assaulted.

Was I? I don't know if I'm entirely sure, even now. On one hand, the narrative of my joke still rings true in my head: *I asked for it.* It was merely a miscommunication. But then, my gut kicks back: NO! No. I did *not* ask for it. I did not, in any universe, ask to be punched in the face. I know some people might be into that sort of thing, but regardless: nothing justifies slamming your hand into a woman's face, unless she literally asks you to slam your hand into her face, and even then, maybe get it in writing before following through, just to be safe. Do a couple of PowerPoint presentations to walk her through the process? How about doing a test on a dummy first so that you're both very clear on what type of punching is good, and what type of punching is not so good? Consider working your way *slowly* toward straight-up violence?

This wasn't miscommunication. Miscommunication is when you tell your lover, "talk dirty to me," and he responds with, "oooh baby, you're so dirty, you're like the floor of an airplane bathroom after a turbulent intercontinental flight." This isn't the type of thing you take a guess at.

The craziest part of the story is what happened after he hit me. He forcefully pushed my face down into the pillow, making it hard for me to talk. I distinctly remember my tongue touching the inside of my front teeth, the way your tongue readies itself to say N, and then, rounding your lips to form the word No. But before I could push the word out, he finished, and suddenly switched into gentleness, creepily kissing me all over my face and neck. It was obvious that he really liked what I had "asked" him to do. In the moment, I thought it was weird, but I didn't feel abjectly unsafe. It all happened so fast—I wasn't sure what to do. Without thinking, I quickly dressed and got the hell out of there.

I woke up the next day, jittery about what had happened. I immediately thought, *What were you thinking? Going into a hotel with a strange person you knew almost nothing about? What if his fetish had been murder?* I felt as if I had narrowly missed getting run over by a bus. I decided to google him, excited to privately mock the douchebag I had managed to land for my coveted one-night stand. The only real information I had gotten about him was his name and that he had a band. *Just enough to find his pathetic Myspace page*, I thought, clicking enter.

But instead of a pathetic Myspace page, I was shocked to see page after page of pictures, news stories, fan sites.

He was *famous*—low-level famous, but famous, nonetheless. *Holy hell*, I thought. I just got punched by a D-list celebrity whom I didn't even know existed, and the reason I didn't know he existed is because he was famous to people much younger than me! I doubled over laughing. On one hand, I had the sexual sophistication of a teenager. On the other hand, I was *too old and out of touch* to know whom I had just fucked.

Even though I still think the story is darkly funny, I have stopped telling it onstage. With time, I could not tell it without thinking about the implications of what had happened. I could not tell it without feeling terrified that someone would find out who I was talking about and turn it into a #MeToo moment against my will. I could not tell it without wondering if I should name him publicly. *What if he hurt others? Young fans? Or maybe I was the only one? And if I was, does that somehow excuse it? Do we really need fifty victims for one to matter? I am fine, though. So why name him? I see how this works—you can't control it once you say it. The world will come for you, which will hurt worse than the original offense. And besides, there is a comedy album out there with you saying the words "I asked for it." You can't change your tune now.*

I shuddered at all of it, and when you're shuddering at your own jokes, the audience can feel it. But it wasn't just the #MeToo movement that changed the story for me. It was also viewing it from a distance and seeing that even though I was adhering to my strict policy of not discussing my past relationship publicly, in a way, I was actually up there telling the story of my divorce. The story of how I believed, in that hotel room, that *this is what you get.*

chapter

nineteen

At lunch on the final day, Bob dropped by once again.

"I would save your life if you fell in," he said.

"Well, I hope so." I chuckled weakly. It was getting harder to stay chill with him, but I figured any other tactic was useless at this point, since we only had one day left.

I told Erin and Ross.

"Gee thanks, Bob. But I'm still not going to have sex with you," I said to them, wishing I had said it to Bob instead.

After lunch, Ted announced that we would make one more stop before our last camp: Pumpkin Spring.

"At Pumpkin Spring," he said, "we've got a big cliff jump directly into the Colorado."

As we traveled downriver, I propped my feet on the outer tube of the raft and let the sun warm my skin. I opened my notebook. I had been writing during calm moments on the river. Whenever we encountered rapids, I would quickly throw it back into its Ziploc bag and tuck it under my life vest. The lyrics for my song were coming together, even though I wasn't sure they were any good.

At one point, I heard a familiar sound, something I had heard several times on the trip already.

"Go sit on it! Try! Just try!" It was Ross's voice on a cellphone video she had taken months earlier. In the little movie, she has just introduced her son Henry to a whoopee cushion. It sits on the floor a short distance away. He is scared of it, eyeing it suspiciously as he hugs her side. With her nudging, Henry finally goes and sits on it. Initially he is afraid to put his full weight on it, but eventually he leans in, the whoopee cushion erupts, and Henry and Ross both dissolve into giggles.

Ross had watched the video several times during the trip. I knew she missed her family so much, and though the video is a classic, what I love about it most is how much her voice sounds like Mom's.

I was definitely feeling Mom down here, but not

through animals or constellations. I was feeling her through Ross.

Of course, I thought. In a way, all four of us had been taking turns embodying Mom since she died, not just in our DNA but in our want to protect and nurture one another.

We came ashore at an impressive stretch of jagged cliffs that featured an odd-looking rounded rock formation. The thirty-foot-wide travertine formation was pale orange, and it actually looked like a giant pumpkin that had been carved out of the limestone; it was filled with a milky aquamarine liquid.

"Don't touch it or drink from it," Matt said, "It's the most poisonous water in the Grand Canyon. Extremely high levels of arsenic." It seemed like the perfect place for aliens to deposit their eggs.

Ted led us up past the pumpkin to a cliff. I couldn't tell how far below us the river was, but if I had to venture a guess, it was somewhere between "no, thank you" and "go fuck yourself." This was an entirely different situation from our cliff jump the day before. This was no tropical kiddie pool—this was twenty thousand cubic feet *per second* of frigid liquid dirt hurtling past us, with maybe a few drops of arsenic mixed in for bonus death.

"Are you going to go first this time?" I asked Ross.

"Hell no," she said.

Ted demonstrated the jump, springing off the ledge like a kid at summer camp. The huge splash he made when he hit the water was evidence that this was a much higher jump than the first. We watched him swim twenty feet downriver to a series of rock steps we would need to use to get out where he had attached ropes for assistance.

I was still shaken from seeing Dan get sucked under, but I was a new person now: I was someone who jumped off cliffs. Two days earlier I was someone who was convinced I would *never* jump off a cliff. I had told Ted repeatedly, "I don't *do* that," as confident as I had been as a teen, telling my peers that I would not be participating in any sort of keg stand or penis touch. But then I had done it—I had jumped! So I could surely pass this much bigger test.

It felt important now that I was on to something: if I could push myself a little harder, leap a little further, anything was possible. Not only athletically (I pictured myself on the cover of *Outside* magazine, ripped and tan, with the headline: "On the Edge: Sara Schaefer's Journey from Comedian to Champion Cliff Diver"), but also professionally. *Maybe it's not over for me.*

"I'm going to do it," I said to Ross, who was still sizing up the situation. Throughout the trip, she had been trying all the scary things first. Now, it was my turn. I marched over to Ted.

"How high is this?" I asked.

"Fifteen feet," he said. "You got this, BoBo. I'll count. One . . . two . . . three . . . JUMP!"

I was still standing there.

"Do it for HENRY!" I heard Ross scream.

"Okay okay okay . . ." I tried again.

"One . . . two . . ."

"NO!" I stepped back from the edge. Vertigo threatened to pull me down into the fetal position. Apparently one cliff dive does not prevent dread from pouring over your body like concrete the next time you try to do it.

Jesus, you are a fucking wizard.

I took in as much air as I could, held my nose, and leapt off the side of that cliff. Everyone cheered, but I couldn't even let out a scream. I waited for impact. But it felt as if it were taking forever. One Mississippi, two Mississippi, three Mississippi . . . *Why am I still in the air?*

Finally, I hit the water, hard. And deep I went, as the Colorado filled my nasal passages and a tiny bit of my lungs. I flailed to reach the top, which seemed so far away. I was underwater for way longer than was desirable, and even though my eyes were welded shut, I could feel how dark it was down there and it spooked me. As I thrashed my way to the surface, I could feel the current already pulling me. *Get to the air, get to the air!* Finally, WHOOSH, I emerged into the sunlight, like a mermaid in all her glory. (Later, when I looked at the video of me jumping, I realized I looked more like a drowning mole.)

Feeling the river push me, I frantically doggy-paddled toward the take out point.

"Help!" I cried, my teeth chattering. I made it to the rope and grabbed on to it. Spandad was there to help pull me up onto the slippery rocks. Fine. He had not helped unload his heavy-ass camera equipment, nor changed his outfit in a week, but at least he helped lift my wet carcass out of the river. Even with his assistance, the climb out was challenging, and I banged my shins several times before getting to solid ground. Eventually, I stood back on top of the cliff. My feet felt like magnets on the stone plateau, as if they were telling me never to do that again.

"Okay, that was . . . *not* the same as the first jump," I said, panting. "But, Ross, you can do it."

Ross got herself in line. This one seemed to scare her as much as it had scared me, and it took her several attempts to make the leap. Her fear made me wonder if I had been almost too brave.

"Don't think! Just jump!" I hollered.

"That's why it's so easy for me and Jesse to jump," Ted said. They had been doing crazy flips and tandem jumps off the ledge between first-timers like us. "We don't have brains. We don't think first."

Ross stepped back to the edge.

"Do it for Hanky!" I said.

She jumped, and when she got out, she was clearly shaken.

"Are you okay?" I asked.

"Yes, it just scared me," she said.

I got a little shiver remembering that brief moment of darkness underwater, that moment of not knowing which way was up.

"But you tried. And you did it!" I said, so glad we had both found the light.

chapter

twenty

On the day I found out MTV had given me a green light, I was in Seattle with my boyfriend, Scott, and I was topless. We had arrived at our friend's house late the night before, and I had insisted we leave our luggage in the car until morning, instead of dragging it down the gravel driveway and waking everyone up. Our pajamas out of reach, we slept in nothing but undies. And so it was, with my tits out, I heard the MTV executive say the words I had been aching to hear.

"It's a go," he announced. "We are ordering twelve episodes!"

"Yes! Yes! Yes!" I pumped my fist in the air, my boobs jiggling with each pump as I chirped. I was so choked up I sounded like a baby lion trying to roar. After I hung up the phone, I kicked my legs around on the bed in glory.

An empty place inside of me—carved out by all the years of second-guessing myself, the rejection, the loss, the doom, the debt, the shame, all of it—was, in an instant, filled. The nasty voice inside my head was buried, and a new one clanged like a bell: *Yes. Yes. Yes.*

The green light from MTV was for *Nikki & Sara Live*, a weekly talk show inspired by the podcast I had been producing with fellow comedian Nikki Glaser. I had made a few minuscule appearances on TV before, but this was a huge leap. This was a whole entire show, with my name in the title, and it was *live*.

On the night of the premiere, Nikki and I stood facing each other in the hallway outside of the studio. We could hear music pumping and the crowd cheering. Sound engineers tucked wires into our collars as wardrobe stylists ran lint rollers over our dresses.

One of us had recently watched a TED Talk in which the speaker said that standing in the "Wonder Woman" stance for ninety seconds was scientifically proven to increase confidence and performance. We decided to try it. We spread our feet shoulder-width apart, puffed out our chests, and put our hands on our hips. I felt powerful, but also as if I might tip over.

Moments later, our stage manager led us into the studio, and we assumed our positions in front of a huge window. This was the old *TRL* studio, with flashy Times Square as our backdrop.

"THIRTY SECONDS!" a voice said on the intercom.

It did not feel real. I tried not to think about Mom, but she had been in my head all day. She would have gone wild over this. I imagined her screaming with joy. It was the best day of my life, pinched by her absence. I felt the low rumble of tears forming in the back of my eyes. *Good God, not now, Sara!*

Just in time, Nikki leaned over and broke me out of my mini-trance.

"Do it for Van!" she said.

I burst out laughing. Van was an executive in the upper reaches of Viacom, the entertainment behemoth that owned MTV. We had never met Van, but he already had a lot of thoughts about our show, which had been communicated to us through a chain of other executives, many of whom we had also never met, who also had their own thoughts about our show.

"Yes!" I said. "Do it for Van!"

"TEN! NINE! EIGHT!"

I took a deep breath. This is not how I expected to experience my first countdown in Times Square.

"SEVEN! SIX! FIVE! FOUR!" Our stage manager started using his hand to complete the countdown. When he made it to one, he waved his finger wildly at the teleprompter. Our dream was now live, beaming into at least a dozen homes across America.

"Hi, I'm Nikki Glaser, and I'm the blonde one!"

"I'm Sara Schaefer, and I'm the one with glasses!"

And so it began.

In our minds, the concept of *Nikki & Sara Live* was simple: we were two funny women with excellent chemistry who loved pop culture, but instead of being fawning robotic entertainment reporters, we would satirize and subvert the celebrity-media machine. This involved flipping traditional red carpets and press junkets on their heads. At the MTV Movie Awards and the VMA's, for example, we competed to see who could gently touch more celebrity arms and shoulders.

At a junket for the animated film *The Croods*, we spent our allotted five minutes with Ryan Reynolds and Emma Stone engaging in awkward small talk. In our minds, junket interviews were already awkward, so why not really lean into it? We knew their publicists would never agree to it, so I had to pitch the idea to Ryan and Emma directly the moment the cameras starting rolling. As we got further into the interview, we could see publicists running about in a panic. After, Ryan happened to catch the same elevator as us, and in it, he continued the bit.

"So . . . this weather, right?"

I am still in love with him to this day.

Another time, we gave two teen girls the shock of a lifetime by smuggling them into a hotel room where, after removing their blindfolds, they realized they were sitting directly across from 2013's most important public entity: One Direction. Viacom Van was disappointed that the girls didn't start crying and make a big show of it; he did not understand that when you are a teenager two feet from Harry Styles's face, your soul leaves your body and you observe the entire incident from above, as a ghost might.

A month later, our showrunner, Kim, secretly used the One Direction segment to convince Justin Timberlake—with whom Nikki and I were deeply obsessed and whom we mentioned on every episode of our show—to give us the same gift. In a hotel conference room in Las Vegas, we sat patiently waiting for what we thought was going to be your run-of-the-mill interview with Ke$ha. But instead, in walked Justin. Yes, I cried, and yes, I was thirty-five years old. But I did not do it for Van. I did it for JT.

At *Nikki & Sara*, all my muscles were engaged. I got to

write, perform, interview, take turns playing the funny lead and the straight-man sidekick, produce, collaborate, strategize, hire, fire, learn, and manage. I did not need the Wonder Woman stance, because I was Wonder Woman already.

But in MTV's minds, our show was something broken that needed to be fixed. They fussed over every little thing and honked new, conflicting directives at us each week. I was curious how a brand-new show that had barely had a second to breathe could be "broken." The ratings were actually pretty good, but I learned very quickly that ratings are like modern art. Everybody sees something different in them, and nobody knows what they *actually* mean.

At one point, MTV's idea of how to "fix" our show was that we should recap the one that aired directly before ours. That show was *Catfish*. Yes, that *Catfish*, a show that combined *To Catch a Predator* with *Cheaters* and added a hipster beard. Recapping it every week on our show was just weird. Kind of like if *The Tonight Show* had to spend the first ten minutes of each episode recapping what had just happened on the local news. And like the local news, *Catfish* was actually an incredibly depressing show. Oh, an episode about a veteran with PTSD who chose to impersonate a rapper online in a desperate bid to find human connection? The jokes write themselves!

It felt gross, but we did the best we could to remain true

to ourselves while also doing as we were told. I feared that if we failed to jump through every hoop MTV threw at us, the entire thing would be yanked away.

I was so afraid of losing the show that I became increasingly obsessed with my own behavior behind the scenes. The negative voice I thought had been buried crept right back in. *Don't become an asshole,* the voice would say. *They'll take the show away. Be a good girl.*

I did everything to avoid becoming a "Hollywood monster." (Over the years, I had learned that in Hollywood, there's a deep divide between public and private. Sometimes a famous person's name will come up, and a quiet blankets the room. And then someone will wearily ask, "Oh no, is he/she a monster?" Sometimes he/she is, and sometimes he/she isn't. Also, a man is a monster if he rapes more than seven hundred women. A woman is a monster if she doesn't smile one time.)

My assistant, Victoria, had to finally ask me to stop apologizing to her every time I needed something.

"It is literally my job to order you lunch," she said. "It is good to let everyone help you and to make you feel comfortable." She was right, because you need to be ready to do your little monkey dance without any distractions. Performing on camera in high-stakes situations is more difficult than it sounds. I am not saying it's as challenging as performing surgery on a baby or influencing others with your Instagram account. But try throwing anyone on live TV while they must simultaneously read a teleprompter, listen to a producer talking into their earpiece, notice a stage manager waving signals at them like an air traffic controller, and oh, here comes Ariana Grande with a live kitten in her hand . . . GO! Also, if you're a woman, there is a litany of other concerns, including boob tape and chin bloat and tooth hue and an attainable, but not *too* attainable, pussy. It takes total concentration.

But still, I kept myself in constant check, and I began to envy Nikki's seemingly carefree attitude. She felt no qualms about stopping production to make sure her makeup looked right. She'd lay down on the floor while we waited for lighting adjustments to take a quick nap. She asked for help when she needed it, and it was fine. Somehow, I didn't believe I deserved the same leeway.

By the end of season two, I had exhausted myself trying to balance it all. As we waited to hear about whether we would get a third season, I analyzed every move I had made. Had I done things *correctly*? Had I made Van proud? Was I a good partner to Nikki? A kind boss to our staff? Surely MTV would realize how valuable two professional, intelligent adult women were for their network. Most of their other on-air personalities were one bar fight away from jail time!

I kept thinking about a conversation I'd had with my family when they flew in for a taping of one of our earlier episodes. I had made sure they got the VIP treatment. At one point during their visit, I got recognized on the street by a pair of strangers. My family practically lifted me off the ground they were so excited. I was so proud to share this experience with them. I wanted to repay them for the love they gave me when I got divorced. I wanted to share this limelight. It was the reward for any bad thing that had ever happened to any of us.

Around a darkened wooden booth in a Manhattan pub, we toasted to my success and talked about how Mom would have just loved this.

"So. You got your dream," Ross said. "What's your *new* dream going to be?"

At the time, the question made my chest expand, and for a moment I forgot about all my little self-imposed rules for good behavior. Anything felt possible.

"I . . . don't know," I said, smiling. "I never thought I'd get this far, it's hard to imagine what could come next."

Now, waiting for judgment from some unknown man high in the network castle, it felt like a dark prophecy. It *was* hard to imagine. Without this show, what would come next?

chapter

twenty-one

The end of our trip grew near. Our final campground, located at river mile 220, was cut in half by a small ravine created by a recent flash flood. Up on the flat sand, huge prickly pear, in full bloom, dotted the foreground against the Redwall Limestone cliffs and dusky sky.

As everyone got comfy for the night, celebratory drinks started flowing. Ross and I had found a spot next to Andrew and Erin, not far from the kitchen. As we sat and applied Aquaphor to our cracked skin, Bob came over.

"Hey, ladies," Bob said. I took in a sharp breath, preparing for whatever horrible joke was on its way out of his mouth. "Do you want me to make you some cocktails? I promise I won't drug them."

"Um, no, we're good," I said through gritted teeth. He moved on, amused with himself. As he walked away, I huffed out an annoyed laugh to the group.

"It's not funny, Sara. I'm fucking triggered." Ross was right—this guy sucked, and it stunk that I couldn't properly express it.

I turned my focus to the impending talent show, which I was dreading. *The song is too corny. Not funny enough.*

I pictured myself in front of the group, performing. I imagined my face, looking sad and wanting.

It made no sense, this sunken feeling. What was I so afraid of? I had already shed my insecurities in front of this group. I had screamed like a banshee through wild rapids and stood frozen in fear at the tops of cliffs. No one mocked me. They embraced me! These were "normies," people who probably shuddered at public speaking and likely wouldn't relish standing on a stage and telling jokes. This was *my* thing.

Up top, in the real world, performing had become procedural for me. Book a show. Promote. Sell tickets. Travel. Hotel. Greenroom. Stage. Lights. Microphone. Moldy beer smells. Laughs. Silence. Smiles. Death stares. More laughs.

Hecklers. Applause. Meet and greet. Merch table. Travel. Bed. Repeat. I could handle it all with detached precision.

But down here, it was all scrambled. I had none of the fixtures that held me up. At the no-talent show, it would not be me, the professional comedian, up there. It would be *me* up there. I would have to let these people see the tiny, barely lit ember inside of me. I feared the blow of their rejection might snuff it out.

chapter

twenty-two

MTV canceled *Nikki & Sara Live* after two seasons. When my agent and manager called to tell me, I had just sat down in a coffee shop with some hot cocoa. I knew immediately by the tone in my agent's voice that it was going to be bad news, so I gathered my things and went outside to find one of New York City's designated crying spots: a park bench.

When they told me the show was over, no tears came.

"Thank you," I said. "Right now all I can feel is gratitude. To have even gotten the chance to make the pilot, much less two seasons? It feels like a miracle."

I was of course sad to not be working with my friends anymore. But I did not allow myself to feel much else. I refused to view any piece of it as failure. This was not a loss; it was a net gain. And even though I described the entire thing as a miracle—a rare success in a business that says "no" 99 percent of the time—I also assumed that it was a miracle that would continue for years on end. Now that I was *in*, I would get to keep making TV shows. There was nowhere to go but up!

The perfect place to go "up" in the entertainment business is Los Angeles, so Scott and I decided to make the move. I was optimistic about my prospects there. I already had a potential book deal, a gig hosting an online aftershow about *Pretty Little Liars*, and a role cohosting an infotainment pilot about how things get made. Of course, I didn't tell anyone about these things, because Hollywood is fickle, and it would be premature to brag about any of it before it was officially available for consumption. I knew the wise thing to do would be to keep it all under wraps . . . Just kidding! I told everybody. I wanted the world to think I was in demand after my stint at MTV and that my life now was basically the opening credits of *The Hills. The rest is still unwritten, bitches.* But within a month of arriving at the hills of Southern California, the book, the aftershow, and the pilot had all vanished.

With no job prospects, I focused on my Authentic LA Life. I bought bespoke vintage pieces for my sun-kissed palatial apartment (palatial, at least, in comparison to the coffins I'd occupied in Brooklyn). I grew vegetables in my backyard to cash in on the guaranteed never-ending sunlight. I purchased a military-grade blender to make sure I was getting my prescribed daily dose of Hollywood pea milk smoothies. I went on *optional* walks! For fifteen years, I trudged the stinky New York streets by necessity—now, walking would be for leisure. (Not to be confused with hiking, another LA pleasure-sport in which you voluntarily walk up a hill in the hopes of seeing a celebrity.) Living in LA was proof that I had made it, proof that things were great.

Nine months later, things were very clearly not great. I'd been working nonstop since middle school. Up until this point, my entire life felt like a rock climb up a cliff face, every inch of me taut, reaching, plotting, scaling, ascending inch by arduous inch, my whole existence balanced on a toe. Now I'd finally gotten to the top and I was walking around on this mesa, relaxed for the first time. But it felt flat. Eerily quiet.

I have tinnitus—for which there is no cure—but you can do things to alleviate the micro-torture. Surrounding yourself with background noise is the number one way to help it. I will forget I have it until I'm in a quiet place: the doctor's office before she comes in the room; the few seconds in my car before I start it; an elevator on the way to a meeting. In that silent space, the ringing is deafening. Metaphorically, this is how it felt after moving to Los Angeles. With the noise of my busy life gone, there was a new noise underneath, one I never even realized was there.

At first, the anxious thoughts felt like my regular episodes of self-doubt. *You are so lazy. Get up and make something funny. Don't be ungrateful. Work harder.* In the past, these negative pep talks would actually light a fire under my ass and get me working. Now, the match was wet, and I couldn't get a spark. I stayed for days on the couch, my brain searching for answers.

I wondered if I was depressed, and decided that maybe I was, but only mildly. Nothing too serious that I couldn't handle it myself. I had read plenty of Twitter threads about mental health and knew what to do. It's easy: you just exercise and keep a gratitude journal.

My gratitude journal was helpful at first, but soon, it started to feel pointless to write over and over that I'm thankful for my tomato plants. Why can't I write about the horrible thoughts I'm having? Oh, I just have to be positive in here? Why is my gratitude journal such a snowflake?

Exercise should have been more helpful than it was. I would shuffle two laps around the Silver Lake Reservoir, but during the entire run I'd just replay incidents from my past, searching for clues, trying to pinpoint where things went awry. It was imperative that I go over every step of my life, reviewing random episodes of pain or humiliation, from recent interactions in greenrooms all the way back to ancient mishaps in childhood. I would study them for information. What wrong choice had I made that time? Once I found it, I would throw it on the steaming pile of *all* my wrong choices that led me to this moment of feeling like dung.

I picked out enemies—anyone who had personally hurt me along the way—especially focusing on the ones who were now becoming wildly successful, the ones who I thought were awful people unfairly rising to glory. I designated them as Hollywood Monsters.

How could someone so bad become so beloved? Doesn't anyone else see the lie? Assholes are not supposed to win. I am a good person—doesn't anyone care?

I would analyze the Monsters' every move, every social media post, each new step in their careers, looking for tells. The sure giveaways that their glittery exterior hid a rotten egg underneath, the proof that their cool-kid vibes were just cheap costumes.

I did not have any such costume. I could not hide who I was from the world. Everyone knew my career was going nowhere. It all felt so unfair and I would start to feel like I was drowning.

Then, I would be watching the eighteenth hour of the *Today* show, and Hoda would read some inspirational quote while sipping from Kathie Lee's signature GIFFT chardonnay, and I would get choked up and decide I'd had enough. I would violently swear my Monsters off. *Attention, asshorns! Your lease is up. Time to move out of my head for good!* No more checking their social media. No more hate-watching their work. No more thinking a single thought about them ever again.

But then I would be driving, and a Monster's face would appear, looming above me, on a huge billboard. In meetings, after shows, in conversations with regular people, the Monsters seemed to be on the tip of everyone's tongues. They were darlings, after all, the talk of the town. I could not escape them no matter how hard I tried.

One day, I was doing my laps, barely hanging on to my sanity. As I rounded a corner, my sneaker landed on a loose magazine page blowing in the wind. I looked down, and it was one of my Hollywood Monsters, staring at me from a fancy photo shoot. This person was going to change comedy, the headline said. This person was *everything*. Their eyes seemed to be looking directly into my soul from that magazine page, saying, *You are nothing.*

The one good thing about running during an anxiety spiral is that you already look like you're crying. People will think that the anguished look on your face is just because exercise sucks (which it does), and that the tears on your cheeks are just sweat beads. Though, I am pretty sure jogging in a state of maximum panic is, according to doctors, "a bit much," and might cancel out whatever health benefits it was supposed to provide in the first place.

I hated how much I focused on my Monsters. I knew it was destructive, but I was obsessed. *I am not crazy*, I told myself, *because I have evidence.* My evidence was the source of my pain: the moments these people had hurt me in the past. One of them had tried to sabotage a career opportunity for me. One of them—someone whose opinion I had once very much respected—told me to my face that I was not a real comedian. *I am not crazy. They were in the wrong.*

But years later, I was holding on to these slights like precious trinkets. They made the stakes real, they gave my anxiety fuel, *they* were the reason my career was going nowhere.

I was not sleeping well. I kept waking up sobbing real tears— something that had never happened to me before. It was the same nightmare over and over: I am home in Virginia, and Mom is there. She is alive. It feels so real, and I am melting with joy. But then, her face changes, and she tells us the cancer has returned. In an instant we know she is going to die again, and I feel the horror of losing her once more, rushing in like a dust storm.

And then I would wake up, choking on grief as intense as the day she died. I hated my brain. It seemed hell-bent on torturing me.

During the day, I was trying to write a television pilot, and I had cleared off the kitchen table and covered it with index cards and books with titles like *The Eight Characters of Comedy* and *The Nutshell Technique* and *Write to TV: Out of Your Head and onto the Screen.*

Spoiler alert: I could not get out of my head.

Every time I tried to start writing, a stampede of bad thoughts would charge in. So instead of writing, I did what every doctor recommends: I spent hours robotically checking social media. I turned my attention to easy morality wars: Women *are* funny! Racism is *bad.* On Twitter, I could fight simple, faceless enemies. But it came with a cost. Social media was rife with triggers about my career (oh look, it's every single living comedian, except for me, hanging out at brunch!), and those "easy" morality wars attracted trolls.

People say you should ignore the trolls, but I am convinced that people who say this have never really been trolled. It's easier to ignore trolls who say generic things like "you're ugly!" or "you're not funny." But when trolls get specific? Good luck.

Around this time, a random guy became obsessed with taunting me on social media. He created dozens of fake accounts for the sole purpose of harassment, and he would do it in the cruelest way imaginable. When I would promote a new show or web series or anything that was meant to be a positive, he would be right there to remind me that my mom was dead. Things like "Another failure. Mom would be so proud," or "Time to find a bridge to jump off so you can finally be with Mom again." Blocking him was useless, because he would just create another account. There was nothing I could do to stop him, and whenever I would think he had lost interest, he would pop up again. For a time, I tried to find out who he was. I wondered if he was someone I knew. The closest I got was luring him into emailing me, from which I obtained his IP address. From the IP address, I was able to determine that he lived in the middle of a state where I had zero personal contacts, which boggled my mind even more. This was a stranger who hated my guts for reasons I have yet to ascertain.

Every time I read any comment from a troll, I did not realize my brain was collecting it, saving it for future use, to add to the withering chorus inside my head. Before long, I was unable to distinguish between what a troll had said to me online and what I believed powerful people thought of me, between what a Monster had done to me and what I had done to myself. It all combined into a singular bitter hymn.

Finally, my boyfriend, Scott, put his foot down.

"I say this out of love for you: You can't live like this. I really think you need to talk to someone."

I absolutely hated the fact that someone who had never been to therapy or been divorced or lost a loved one was telling me to go to therapy. But I knew he was right and called a therapist that afternoon. She asked me what was going on.

"I . . ." I immediately started crying. "I just can't stop the negative thoughts."

"It's okay," she said gently. "We're going to get you some relief."

My new therapist was the first person to give my situation a name: anxiety. Unlike my therapists from the past, I completely committed to this one. Together, we worked on separating thoughts from feelings and public from private, and she showed me that living in the in-between—that gray area between black and white, between grand perfection and abject failure—was possible.

From that point, I was able to slowly remove the shackles

and create again, and in the next few years, I had many small victories. For the first time in my career, I was making real money doing stand-up comedy, and I also was getting consistent work writing for television shows. I landed a few development deals, but none of them made it to air. Much of my best work never saw the light of day. But I was working, and that was something.

I was still a work in progress, though. Even with this newfound understanding of my anxiety, and even with the work I'd done with my therapist, I still sometimes clung to my old narrative, and would feel injustice anytime my straight-and-narrow path did not lead to career highs.

I could not admit to myself that losing my MTV show hurt me as much as it did. I knew loss: a marriage, a mother, my innocence when Dad confessed all those years ago. The loss of a silly comedy show, in which we made jokes about Justin Bieber's pet monkey, did not seem worthy of my grief, so I had never allowed myself to feel it.

But with every year that passed, every rejection pushed me further and further away from that one glimmering moment, and the empty place in me that MTV had filled grew cavernous once again. I had to ask myself, *What is it that I want?* I had to be honest. *I want that feeling again.*

I wanted to be Wonder Woman again.

Meanwhile, Nikki kept getting more shows, more opportunities, more famous. Unlike my Hollywood Monsters, Nikki inspired me, and I always rooted for her.

"Your success is my success," I used to tell her at MTV, anytime we realized we were feeling competitive with each other. We would talk often about how our business pitted women against each other, how we had been conditioned to feel threatened by each other's accomplishments. We were taught that there is "only room for one." We decided that we were stronger together, and it has served us both well ever since.

But I would be lying if I didn't admit that I would sometimes collapse into tears upon hearing of another big step up in Nikki's career, worrying about the way it all looked in comparison to mine, and what it all meant.

The trolls must have gotten wind of this (trolls are not psychic, but their own cozy relationship with pain enables them to accurately guess at yours), because they started leaving me heat-seeking-missile-like comments, such as "You're just bitter because Nikki went on to be successful and you're not," or "Well now we know who the real talent of that duo was."

Now, five years out from MTV, I worried they were right. Did I have any talent at all? Or was it all just a fluke? Was any of that success actually mine? Or was I a thief?

I anointed these questions and made them rulers over my life. They demanded conference anytime I had a new dream appear in my mind. *Best not to even try,* I thought. *Your moment has passed.*

And then, I climbed onto a light-blue raft on the Colorado River.

chapter

twenty-three

As the sun went down, everyone gathered around Ted's soup-can lantern for dinner, and then, it was time for the no-talent show.

It was a variety show in the truest sense: Spandad's tween daughter sang a song she made up. Erin performed a Shakespearean monologue from memory, while seated in her chair, and something about her remaining rooted there gave it even more power, and I was blown away. Ross rapped every single word of "Rapper's Delight," which, in case you're not familiar, is challenging because it has ten verses. Andrew delivered a hilarious presentation about his hat and all of its hidden functions.

Finally, it was time for me to sing my song. Ted and I had worked out a melody for it earlier. We had decided that the verses should be spoken, in a sort of old-timey campfire way. The chorus would be sung like an Irish drinking song.

Ted started strumming, and I stood nervously, the lantern lighting my face. The performer in me, still there somewhere, took over, and I began:

Well we started down the river at Lee's Ferry

A group of total strangers numbering twenty

Ted was our captain on this chocolate stream

He told us tales and drove the boat and told us
    where to pee

On boat two was a brown-haired dude by the
    name of River Daddy

Matt's blonde locks blew in the wind as he taught
    us geology

And there was this random guy who was friends
    with Teddy

His name was Earthworm . . . but we called him
    Jesse

Some of the rapids were just a tiny little splash

And some of them were a wall of water that
    knocked me on my ass
They had names like Georgie and told us tales of
    the past
And they took us from boiling hot to icy cold in a
    flash . . .

The song was already killing. I could tell everyone loved
it. Then, Ted joined me for the chorus.

We ran the river and we ran it just fine
And I'm just so glad that nobody died
Know the canyon's history, study rocks made by
    time
When I think of the canyon, I get a tear in my eye.

I sang another verse with specific references to funny
moments on the trip. I looked around and saw everyone's
faces flickering and joyful. After singing the chorus again, I
hit them with my final verse.

Thank you to our river guides for this incredible
    journey
Your expertise and kindness kept us all off the
    gurney

The change in me I may not know for weeks
But the shift I can feel will be tectonic and deep
The canyon may be a crack in our earth's very skin
But it's somehow healed the brokenness within
Years from now when I think of this trip
I'll think of all of you . . .
    . . . and a beefy naked man sitting on a cliff taking
    a shit.

When I started the final chorus, I was thrilled to hear everyone joining in.

We ran the river and we ran it just fine!
And I'm just so glad that nobody died!
Know the canyon's history, study rocks made by
    time . . .
When I think of the canyon, I get a tear in my eye.

"One more time!" Ted shouted. We sang it all together again, and when it was over, the entire group erupted in applause. I sat down, gleaming.

The show kept going, with some folks giving heartfelt speeches. Andrew and Erin sang a song together, and lastly, the guides performed a skit straight out of the camp counselor textbook, one that involved Jesse slathering food and toothpaste and other items all over Matt's face. Even though this was humor meant for teenagers, it tickled me to my core.

When the show ended, we all stayed in our circle, sharing and giggling long into the night. At one point, I noticed Bob was completely tanked, which did not surprise me, because he had announced earlier that he was trying to finish all the alcohol he had brought on the trip. From what I could tell, he seemed to not be bothering anyone, so I stopped worrying about him. Finally, people peeled off from the circle one by one, retreating to their cots for a final slumber under the stars.

Just as I was falling asleep, Ross pushed on my back, whispering.

"Sara. Sara? Wake up," she said.

"What is it?" I mumbled, eyes still closed.

"It's Bob. He's acting really crazy," she said. "He's over there, sitting right by Erin's cot! He's making insane sounds and going like this!" She waved her arms up and down. I looked over her shoulder. I could see Bob's face lit up by an iPad. He had a wild look in his eyes.

"What is he doing?" I was still confused. Ross was already getting up.

"I think he's having some kind of breakdown. I have seen this before. He might do something crazy. I'm going to wake up the guides."

Ross walked down to the river.

"HUGAAH!" I heard a man's voice. It was a strange combination of a growl and a moan, and it was Bob.

I looked down to the river, and I could see the light of a flashlight bobbing up and down as Jesse and River Daddy got off the boat to talk to Ross. I watched as they went over to Bob and coaxed him back to his cot. Ross came back to our tent.

"They are putting him to bed," she whispered.

"Okay, good," I said. "Thank you, Rossy."

I was relieved she had noticed his behavior, and shuddered thinking of what might have transpired if she hadn't taken care of it. I turned over and tried to return to sleep. But a minute later, I felt Ross tap my shoulder once again.

"Sara," Ross whispered again, this time laughing. "Can you hear him?"

I listened but heard nothing.

"He's howling like a sad wolf!"

I listened again, and could barely make out the sound of a grizzled man softly howling at the moon. It was the saddest thing I'd ever heard, but it was also hilarious.

"Oh my god, Ross, what the hell?"

"Awooooo!" Ross howled back, as quietly as she could. Her attempts to do it quietly so as to not wake up anyone else made me laugh even harder. The laughing grew. My entire cot was shaking, and I could not calm myself down. Every time I caught my breath, I would think of the howl and I lost control all over again. Ross kept laughing with me, until she was too exhausted and fell asleep.

But I could not stop. I stared at the moon, barely able to breathe, tears streaming down my face. Now I didn't know what I was laughing at. It was that kind of laugh that releases every endorphin into your bloodstream and leaves you limp like a rag doll on the floor. That kind of laugh that expels every negative feeling you've ever had. I wasn't thinking about anything at all and I laughed and laughed until my abdomen ached. Something had grabbed me, holding me on this frequency until I could take no more. In a way, I, too, was howling at the moon.

And in that moment, it happened. The Grand Canyon completely took me apart. There was nothing left. It had all come out of me right there in one long, uncontrollable laugh.

Empty, I stared at the rock walls standing guard all around us, immovable, like Shelly's makeup, and eternal, like Spandad's outfit.

I thought about the no-talent show, and smiled at how well it went. I felt so relieved and grateful. I flashed back to River Daddy suggesting we do it in the first place, just so I could have an excuse to perform. He called it a no-talent show on purpose, so I would not have to feel any added pressure. He carved out a space for me to show everyone who I was.

He and the other guides hadn't just nudged me to leap off literal cliffs, they had nudged me to take a leap of faith on myself. As tiny and insignificant as my river song was, it now felt as if it had saved my life. As if it had pulled me out of a churning river just in time.

I originally thought I had come down here to face my physical fears: water, boulders, scorpions, pooping into a can. But 220 miles later, I had seen marble and lava and lizards and sheep and moss and sand. I had seen entire ancient oceans reduced to stripes on a canyon wall. I had seen a billion years of change in a pebble.

I had joined the torrent of mud and rock and tree and feather and bone. I had tumbled through a canyon made by us, made of us. The river carried me, and when it was done, it spit me out into the moonlight.

acknowledgments

Thank you to Lauren Spiegel for nudging me off the cliff (get it?) to tell this story, and to Rebecca Strobel for your thoughtful guidance throughout. I apologize to you both for crying so much. Cait Hoyt, thank you for having my back, and to Kara Welker, I am so glad you are my ever-present good witch. Luke Dempsey, what can I say? You saved me from the Doom. Thank you to Carla Benton, Sherry Wasserman, Paige Lytle, and Sara Kitchen for your top-notch work.

For their feedback, support, good ideas and even better catches, I am so grateful to Kim Armstrong, Lisa Curry,

Mary Beth Huwe, Rachel Thompson, and Amy Miller. For their kindness at key moments, thanks to C.C. Hirsch, Audrey Rowe, Tyler Amato, Mike and Mimi Weaver, Laila and Al Dawson, Marina Shifrin, Charla Lauriston, Diana Dinerman, Lindsay Robertson, Andrew Montgomery, Erin Hart, Courtney Stevenson, Lauren Reeves, Heather Havrilesky, Erin and Doug Renard, and the good people at Silver Lake Coffee. Winnie Flach, I don't know if I could have done this without your expertise and empathy.

Thank you to everyone at Grand Canyon Whitewater, especially Ted, Tyler, Matt, and Jesse, for making me a river runner and so much more.

Annie, Pete, Dee, Aaron, Shaun, and Phedra: thank you for being a part of my family. Max, Chloe, Will, Nate, Abe, Jana, Josie, and Henry: please don't read this book until you are seven hundred years old.

Dad, Jay, Cristy, and Ross: everything I write here just sounds corny and inadequate, so instead I will borrow these wise words from Mom: "Raw leather raw leather." Just kidding. I love you all so much it hurts. No amount of Pound Puppies could compare to the gift you gave me: your trust in me to tell this story. Dad, our conversations about this project have been life-changing. Jay, I could fill an entirely separate book with all the ways you've made me laugh and feel protected. Cristy, my favorite color is still orange and I can't wait to eat a celebratory beast feast with you. Rossy, if it weren't for you, I wouldn't have gone down into that canyon. You are kind. You are beautiful. You are bean.

Scott, thank you for having the guts to really know me and remain by my side. I'm sorry I didn't let you write your own Pearl Jam–themed chapter. The editors were really on my ass about it.

about
the author

Sara Schaefer is a stand-up comedian and writer. She was the cohost of MTV's *Nikki & Sara Live* and has written for numerous television shows, including *The Fake News with Ted Nelms* and *The Kennedy Center Mark Twain Prize for American Humor*. Sara's solo show *Little White Box* debuted to a sold-out run at the 2017 Edinburgh Fringe Festival, and her *Comedy Central Stand-Up Presents* special premiered in 2019. She lives in Los Angeles.